WINTER 2020

IN THIS ISSUE:

SUMMER PARADISE IN THE HEART OF HUDSON VALLEY | P.3

A HISTORIC HUDSON VALLEY FARMHOUSE REINVENTED BY DUNCAN AVENUE DESIGN STUDIO | P.12

DESIGN YOUR KITCHEN LIKE A MILLENNIAL | P.27

#FITLIFE COVER STORY WITH SOPHIA MARTELLY | P.36

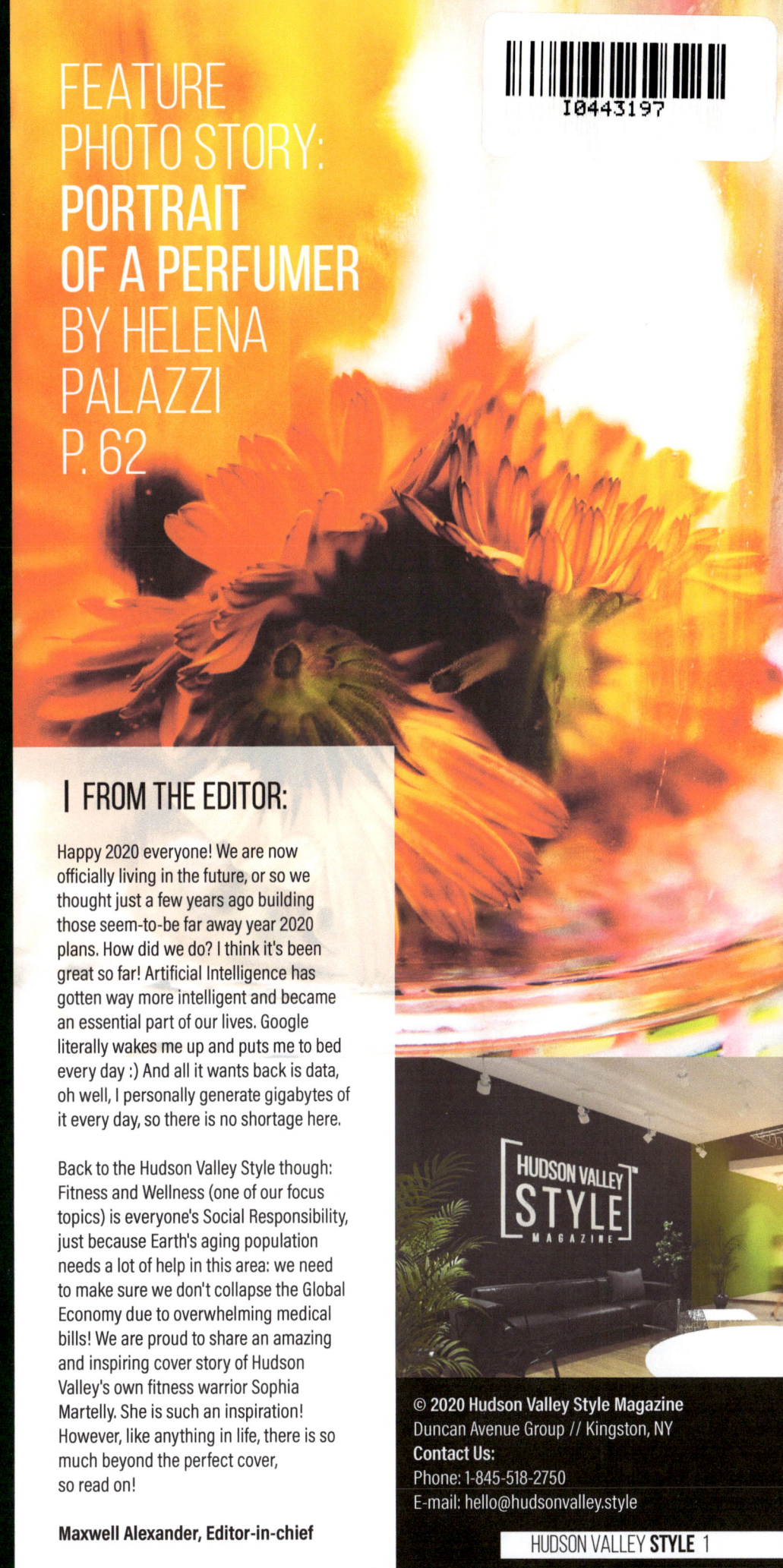

FEATURE PHOTO STORY: PORTRAIT OF A PERFUMER BY HELENA PALAZZI
P. 62

FROM THE EDITOR:

Happy 2020 everyone! We are now officially living in the future, or so we thought just a few years ago building those seem-to-be far away year 2020 plans. How did we do? I think it's been great so far! Artificial Intelligence has gotten way more intelligent and became an essential part of our lives. Google literally wakes me up and puts me to bed every day :) And all it wants back is data, oh well, I personally generate gigabytes of it every day, so there is no shortage here.

Back to the Hudson Valley Style though: Fitness and Wellness (one of our focus topics) is everyone's Social Responsibility, just because Earth's aging population needs a lot of help in this area: we need to make sure we don't collapse the Global Economy due to overwhelming medical bills! We are proud to share an amazing and inspiring cover story of Hudson Valley's own fitness warrior Sophia Martelly. She is such an inspiration! However, like anything in life, there is so much beyond the perfect cover, so read on!

Maxwell Alexander, Editor-in-chief

© 2020 Hudson Valley Style Magazine
Duncan Avenue Group // Kingston, NY
Contact Us:
Phone: 1-845-518-2750
E-mail: hello@hudsonvalley.style

almaxrealty™
[ALEXANDER MAXWELL REALTY]

LOG ON TO ALMAXREALTY.COM TO JOIN US ON A JOURNEY OF TAKING HUDSON VALLEY REAL ESTATE TO NEW HEIGHTS!

WE DO MORE

SUMMER PARADISE IN THE HUDSON VALLEY

| PHOTO STORY
BY MAXWELL ALEXANDER

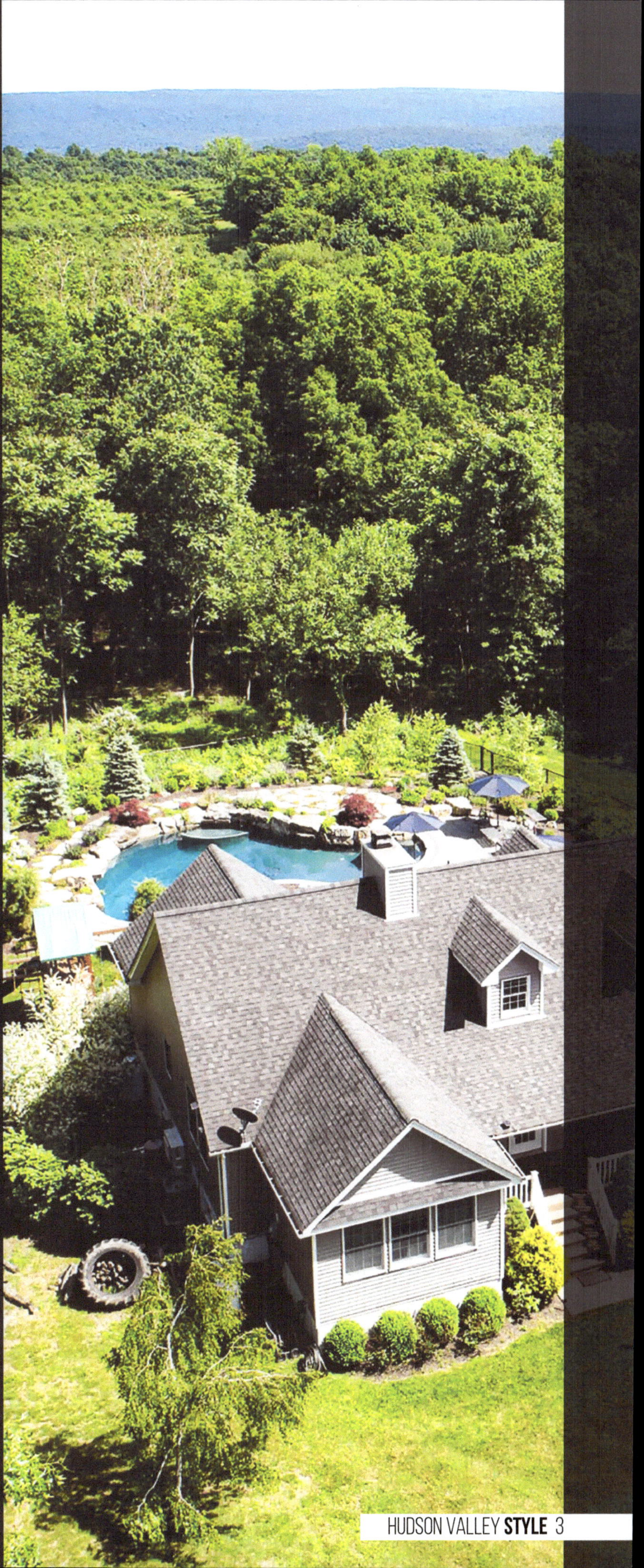

This photoshoot literally took more than 6 months to accomplish, just because summer is not a permanent thing in the Hudson Valley. In fact, I know a lot of people who weather the winter months in warmer climates such as Florida in the US or Caribbean Islands for those who are even luckier.

Well, for those who can still bear the snow and frigid temperatures here in the Modern Rustic Capital of the World, we can only dream of the warmer weather, so please enjoy this warm and fuzzy photo story from Rock Tavern, New York!

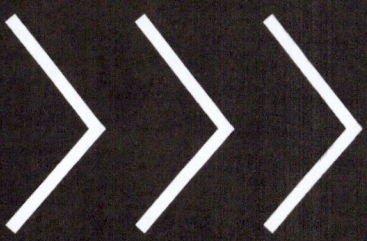

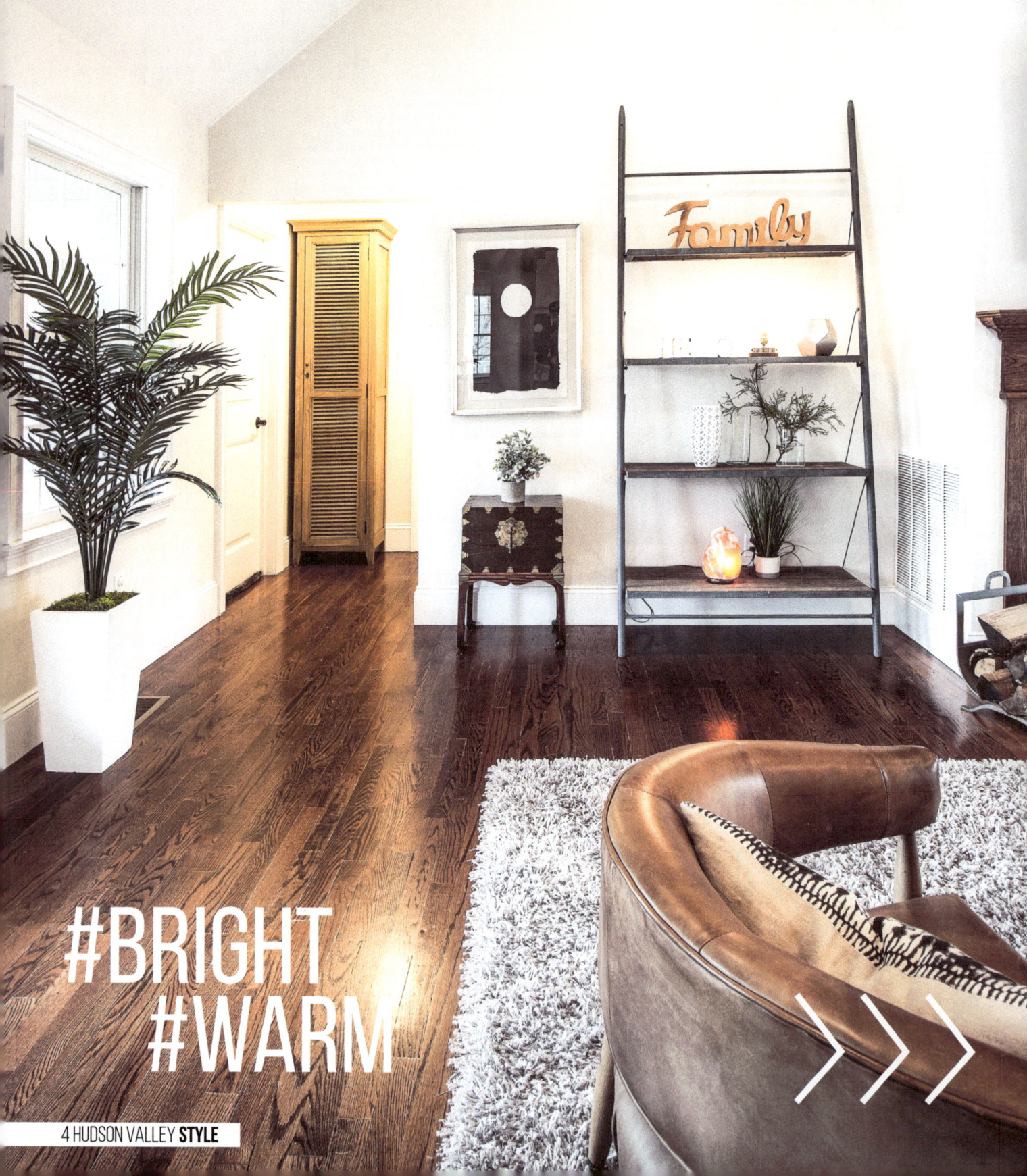

SUMMER PARADISE IN THE HUDSON VALLEY
PHOTO STORY BY MAXWELL ALEXANDER

#BRIGHT
#WARM

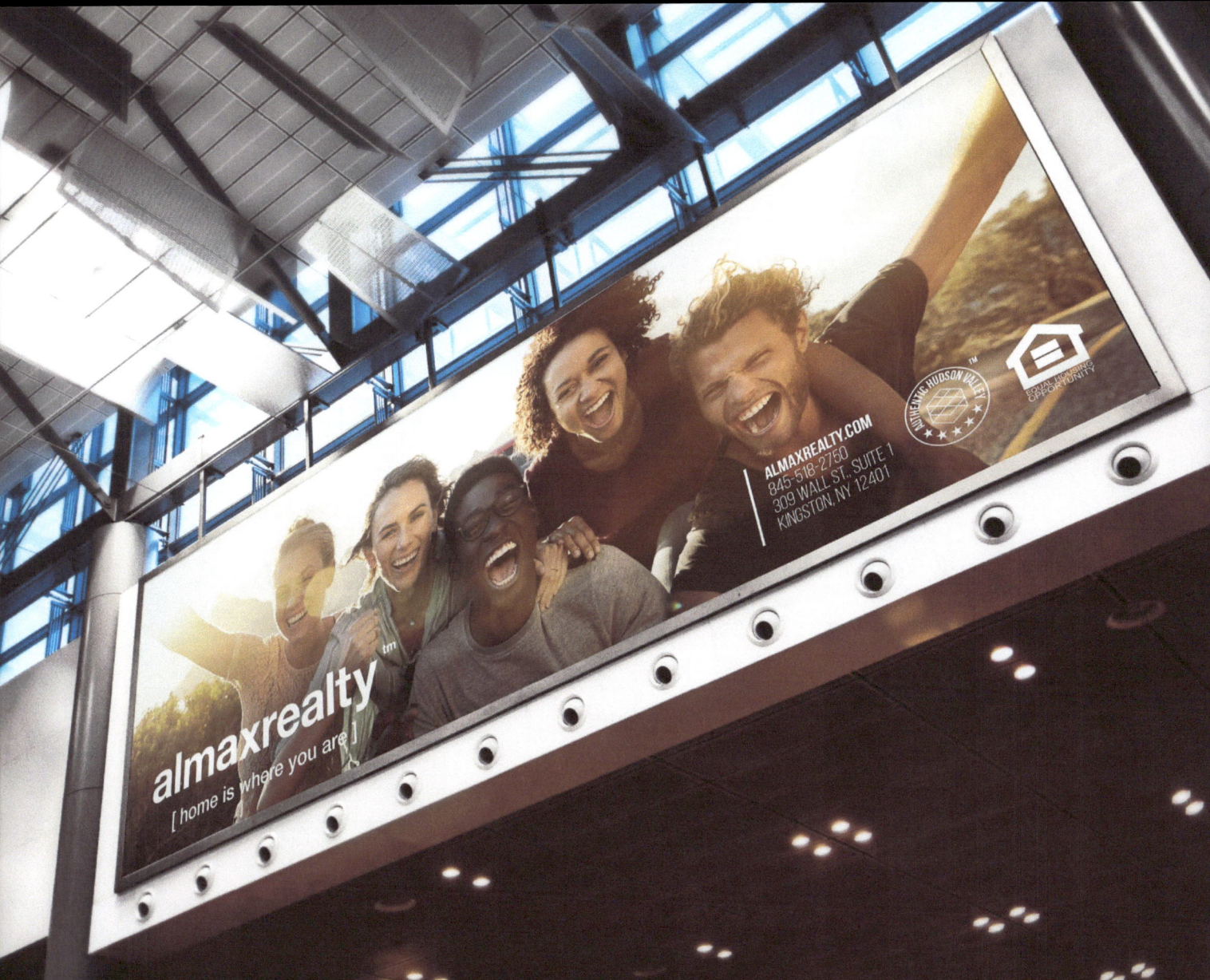

ALEXANDER MAXWELL REALTY™
WORK WITH THE BEST REAL ESTATE AGENTS
IN THE HUDSON VALLEY

If you are looking to sell or buy a home in the Hudson Valley, you should work with the best real estate agents in the Hudson Valley! Alexander Maxwell Realty provides complimentary award-winning real-estate photography and a world-class strategic marketing package with every listing. We are not just the best at selling homes but we go beyond than most by bringing our expertise and experience in real estate investment, interior design, marketing, home staging, renovations & remodeling, and much more.

BUILDING ROBUST PARTNERSHIPS
When you choose Alexander Maxwell Realty you choose the best Team of Hudson Valley Realtors. We transcend conventional real estate services and offer our own touch of creativity and high-end design to any project we undertake and along the way we unleash our own creative genius and professional expertise to your benefit. We aim at developing long-standing relationships with all of our valued clients, like you, and we offer services to match your expectations of us. An important part of these relationships is being able to put to use the very best in technology and industry tools to your advantage.

Log on to **almaxrealty.com** to learn more.

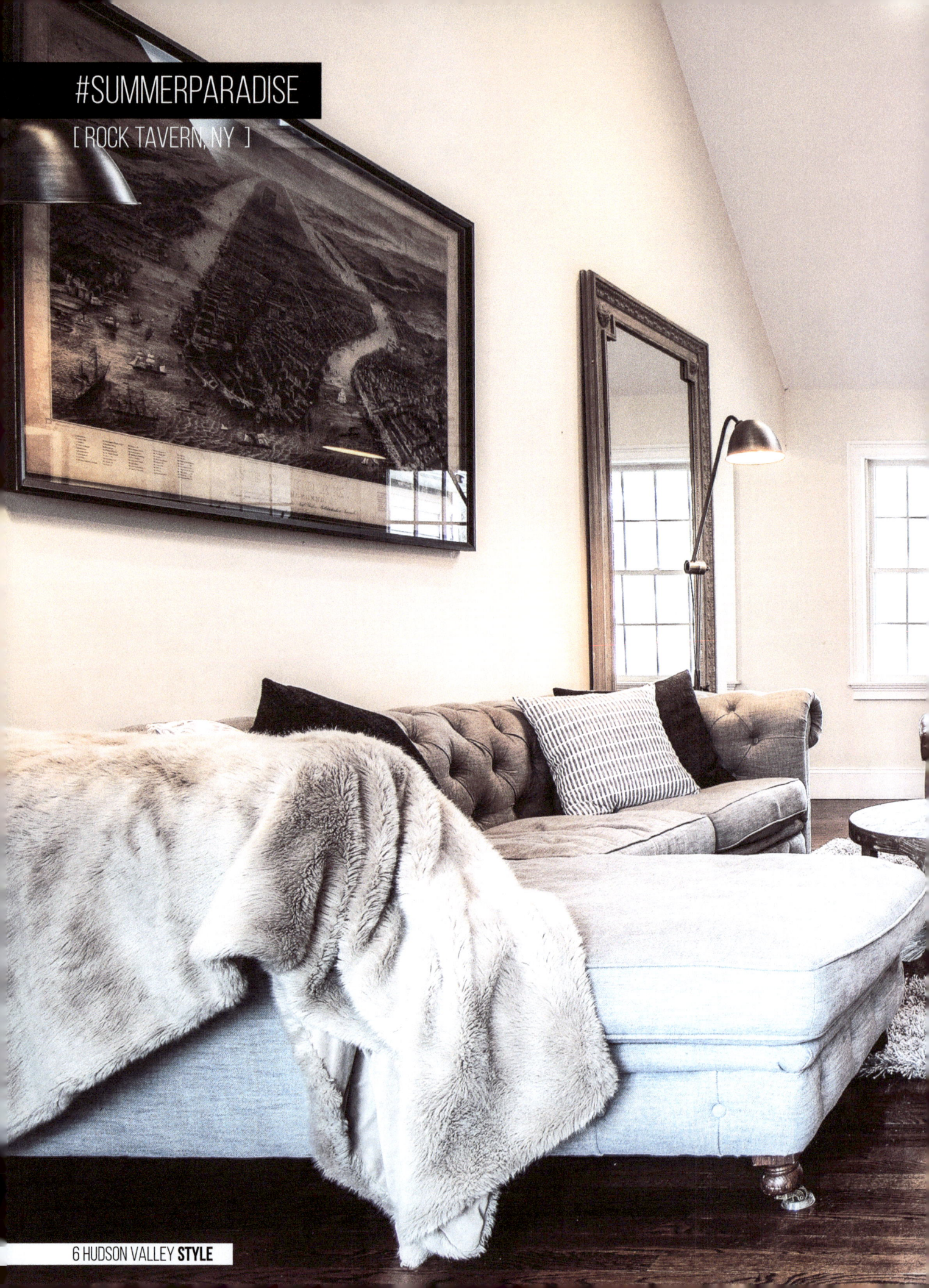

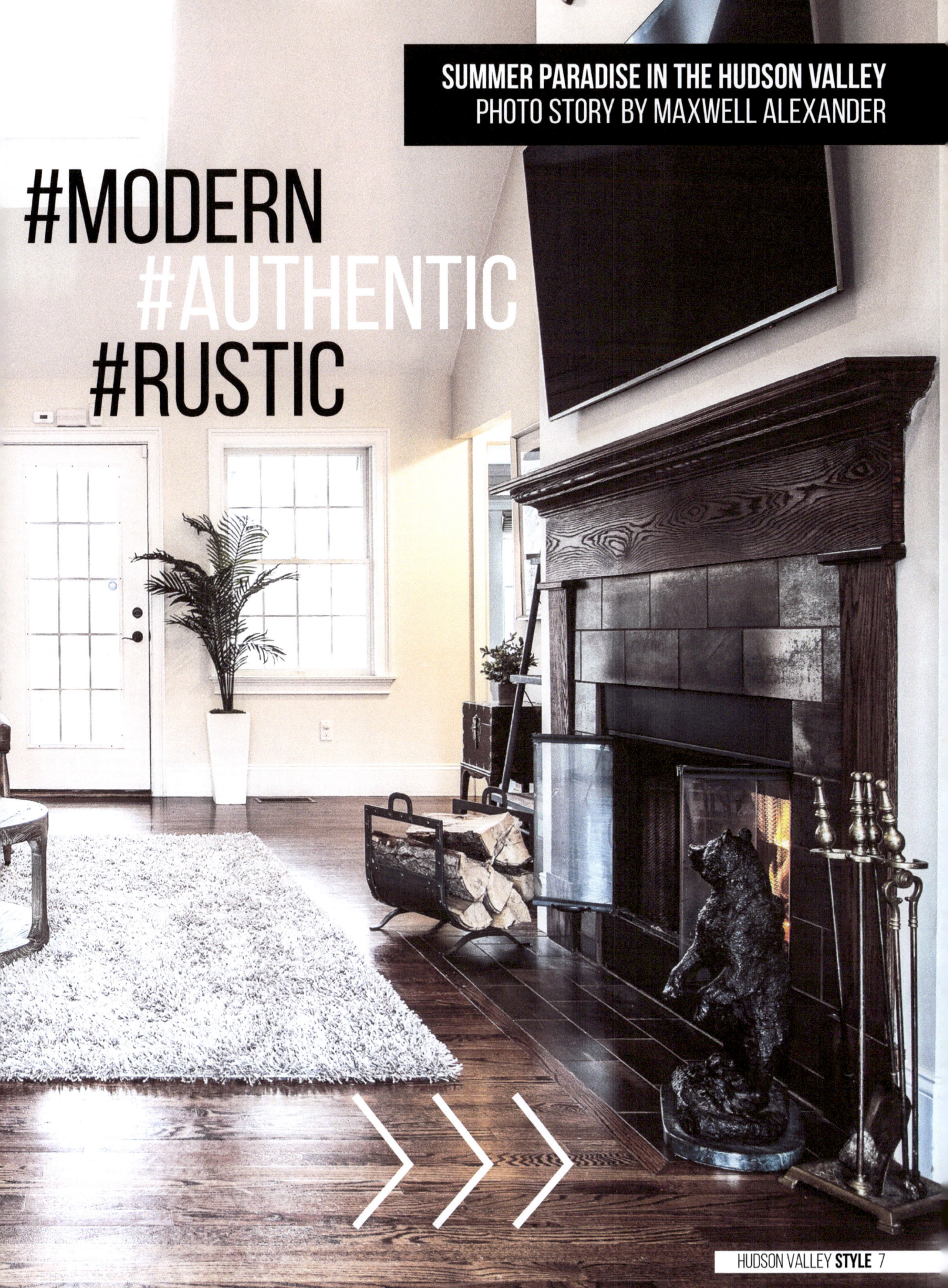

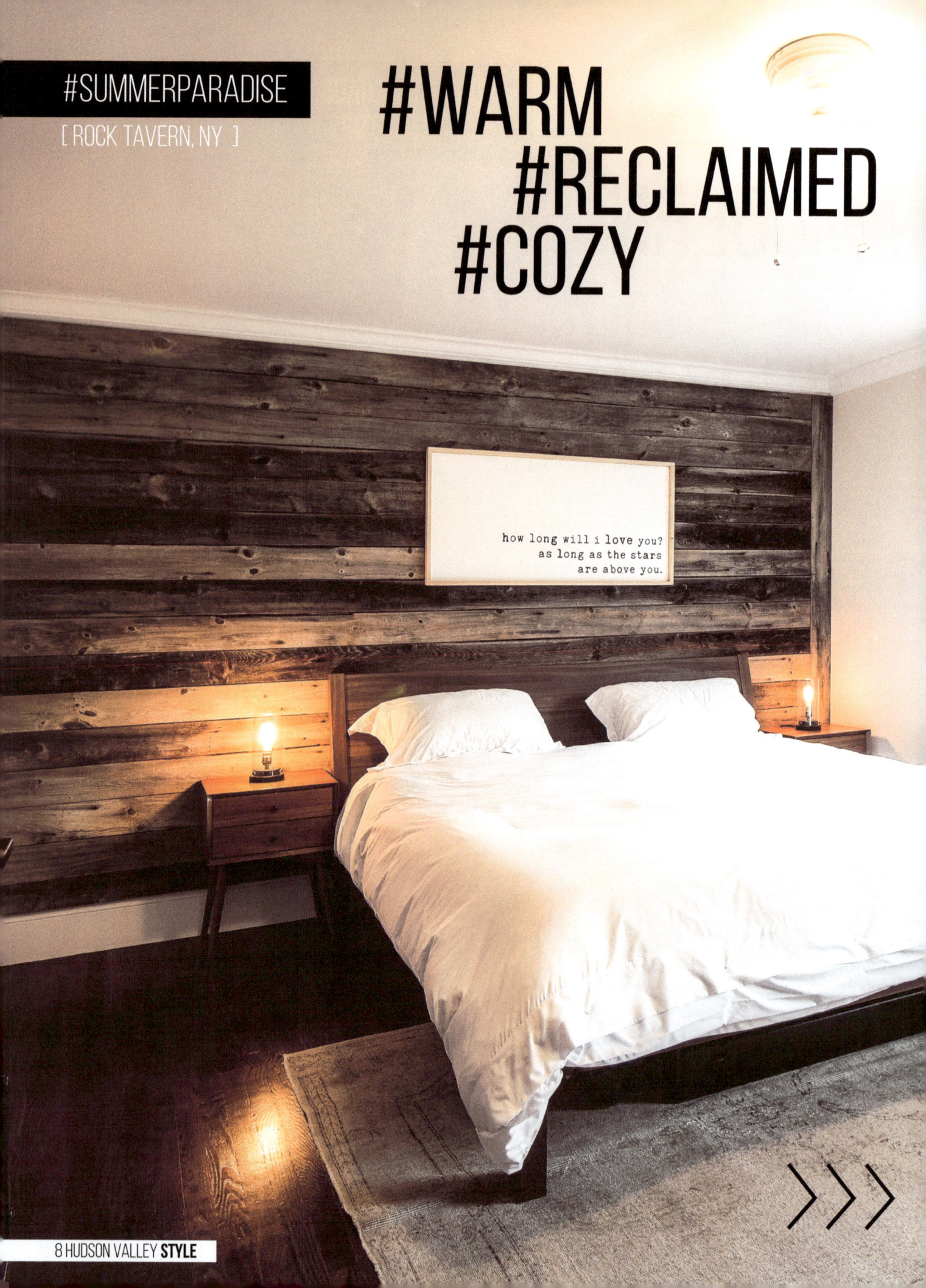

SUMMER PARADISE IN THE HUDSON VALLEY
PHOTO STORY BY MAXWELL ALEXANDER

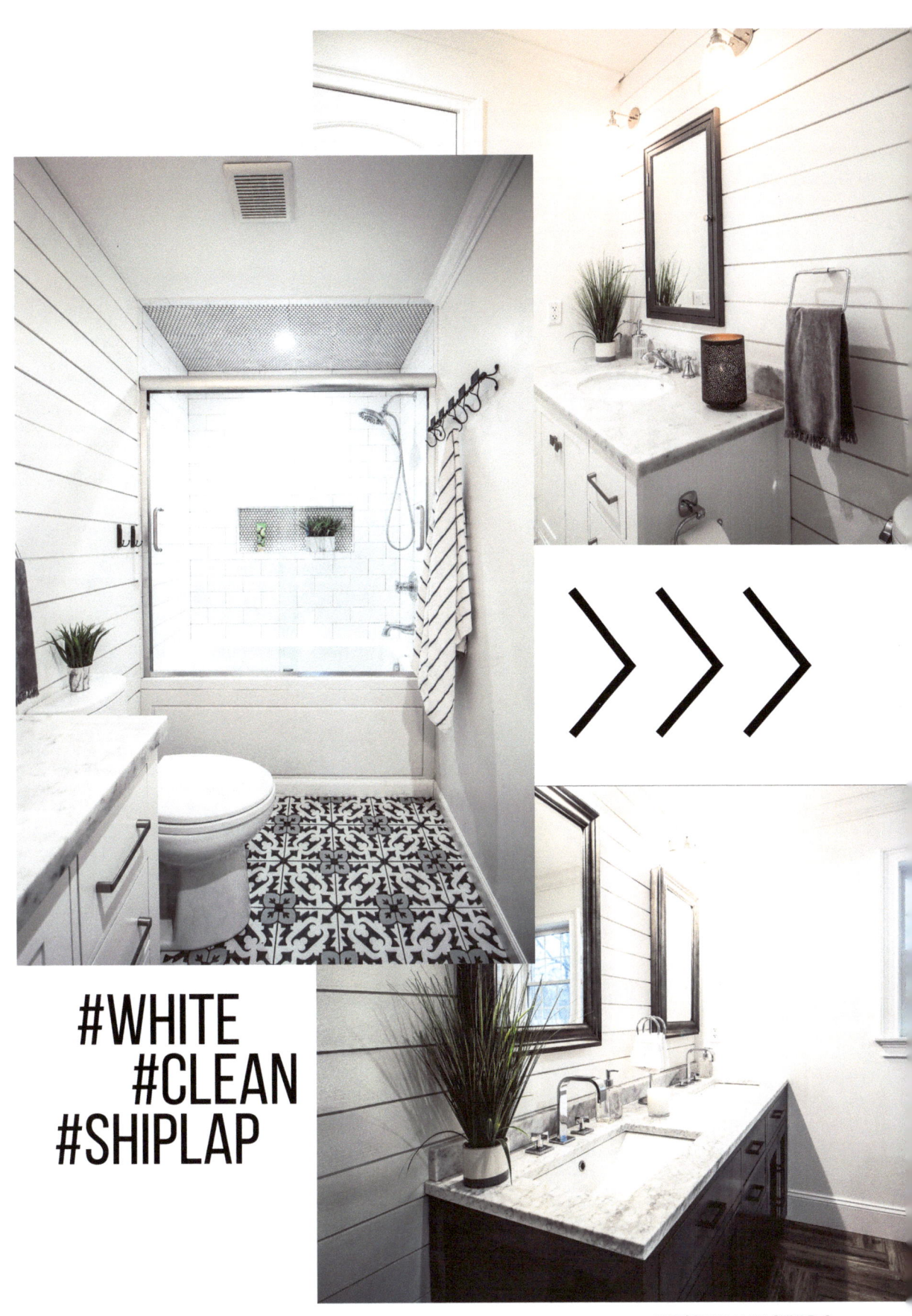

\#WHITE
\#CLEAN
\#SHIPLAP

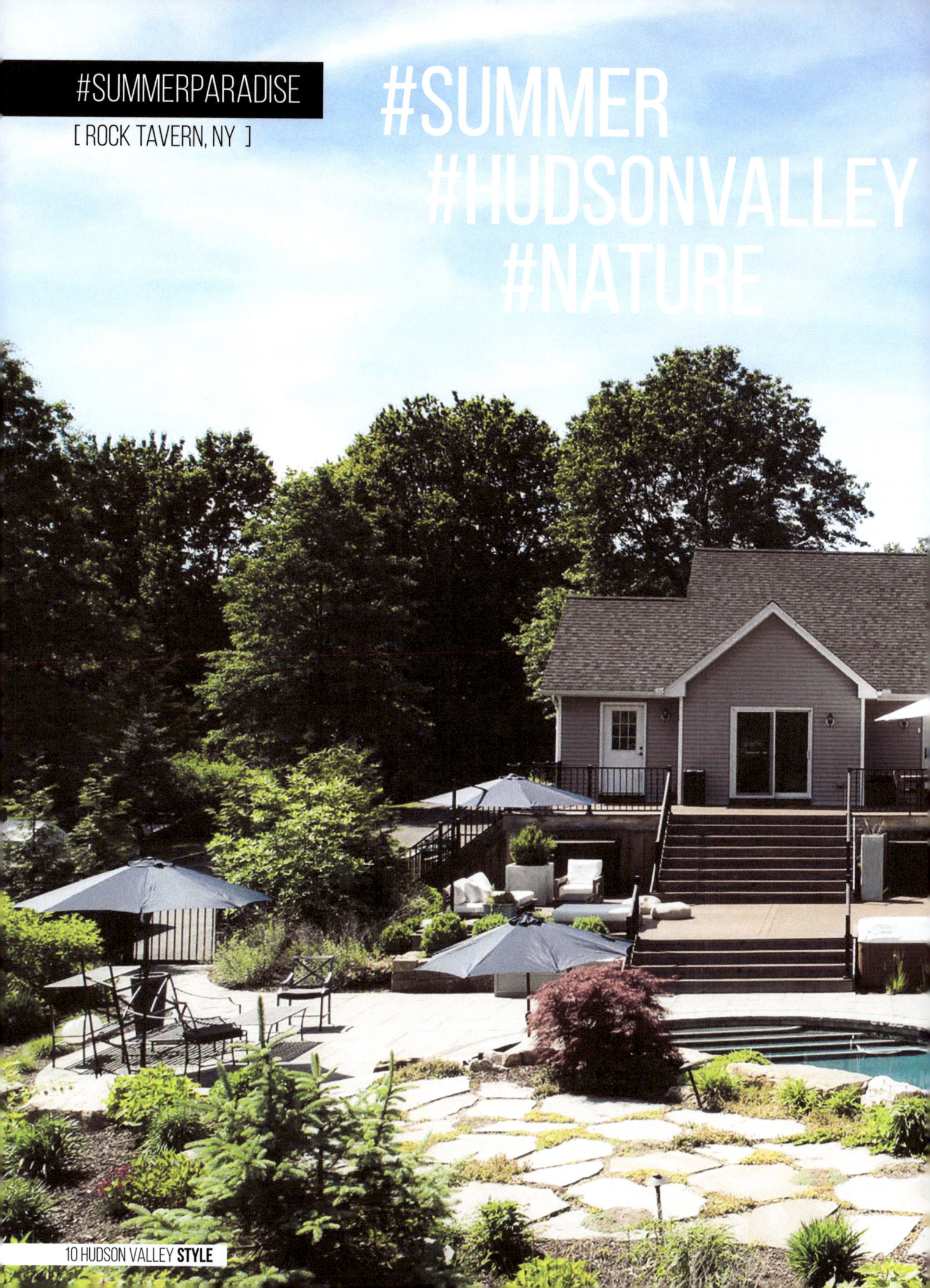

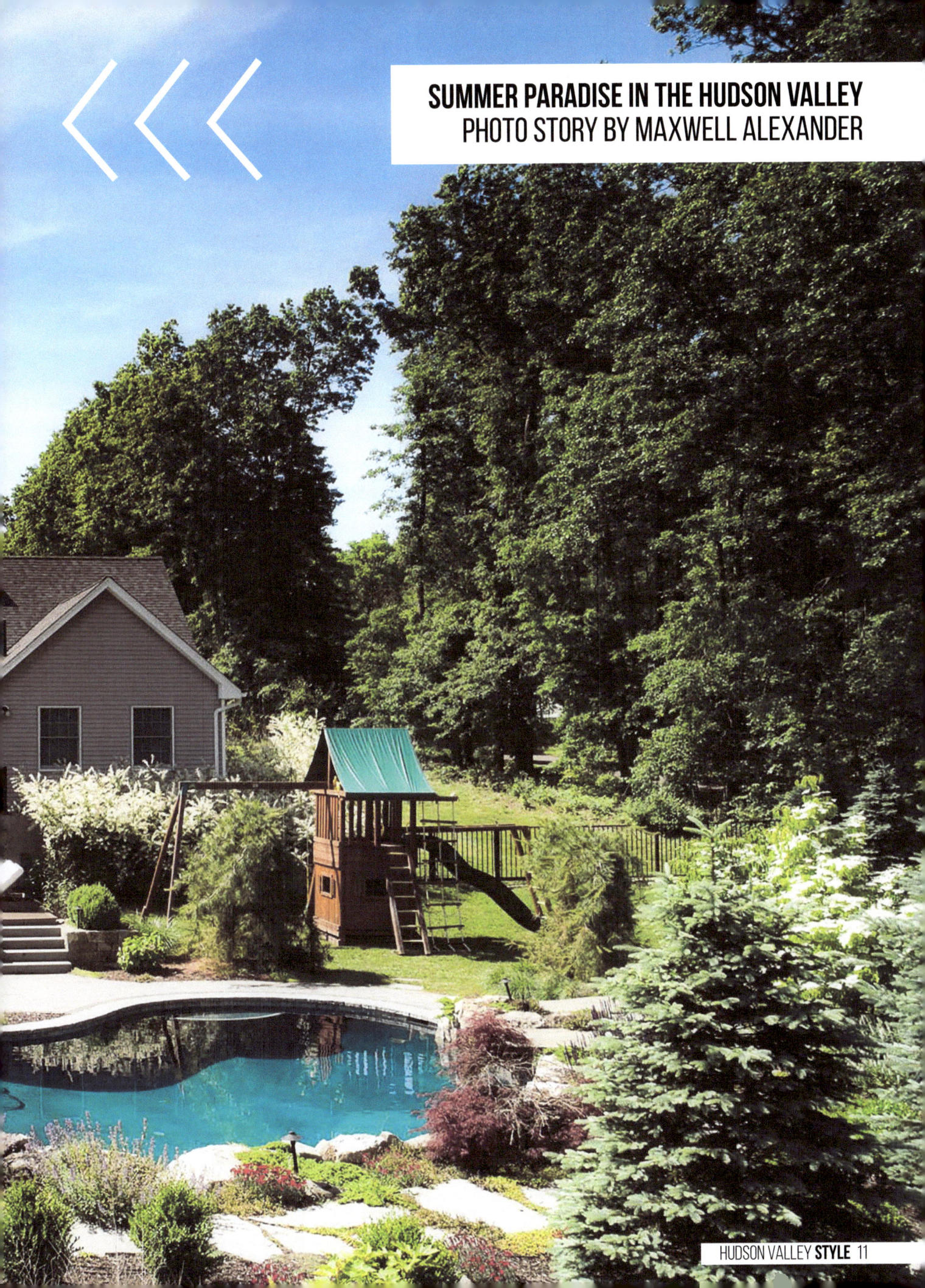

SUMMER PARADISE IN THE HUDSON VALLEY
PHOTO STORY BY MAXWELL ALEXANDER

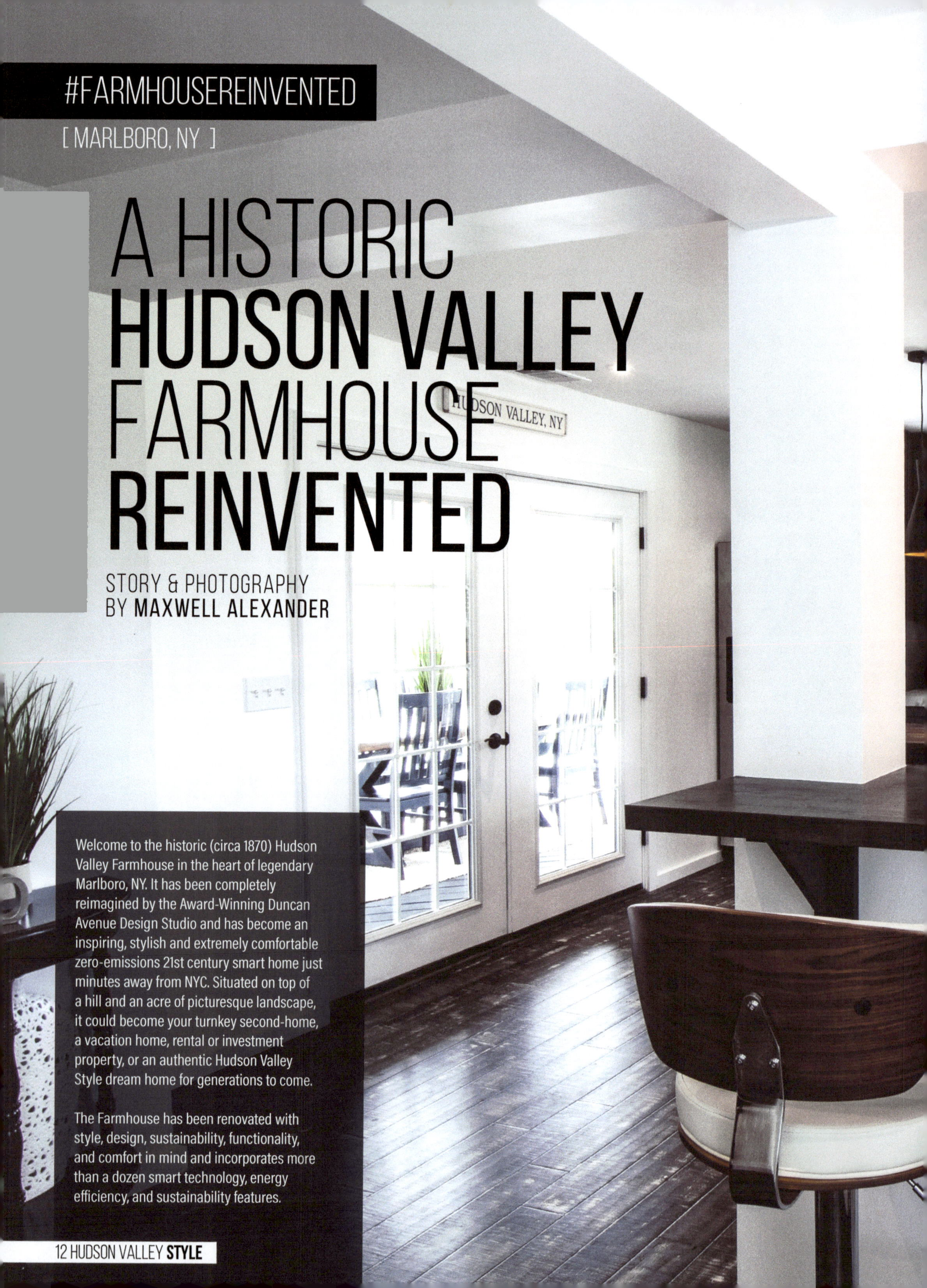

#FARMHOUSEREINVENTED
[MARLBORO, NY]

A HISTORIC HUDSON VALLEY FARMHOUSE REINVENTED

STORY & PHOTOGRAPHY BY **MAXWELL ALEXANDER**

Welcome to the historic (circa 1870) Hudson Valley Farmhouse in the heart of legendary Marlboro, NY. It has been completely reimagined by the Award-Winning Duncan Avenue Design Studio and has become an inspiring, stylish and extremely comfortable zero-emissions 21st century smart home just minutes away from NYC. Situated on top of a hill and an acre of picturesque landscape, it could become your turnkey second-home, a vacation home, rental or investment property, or an authentic Hudson Valley Style dream home for generations to come.

The Farmhouse has been renovated with style, design, sustainability, functionality, and comfort in mind and incorporates more than a dozen smart technology, energy efficiency, and sustainability features.

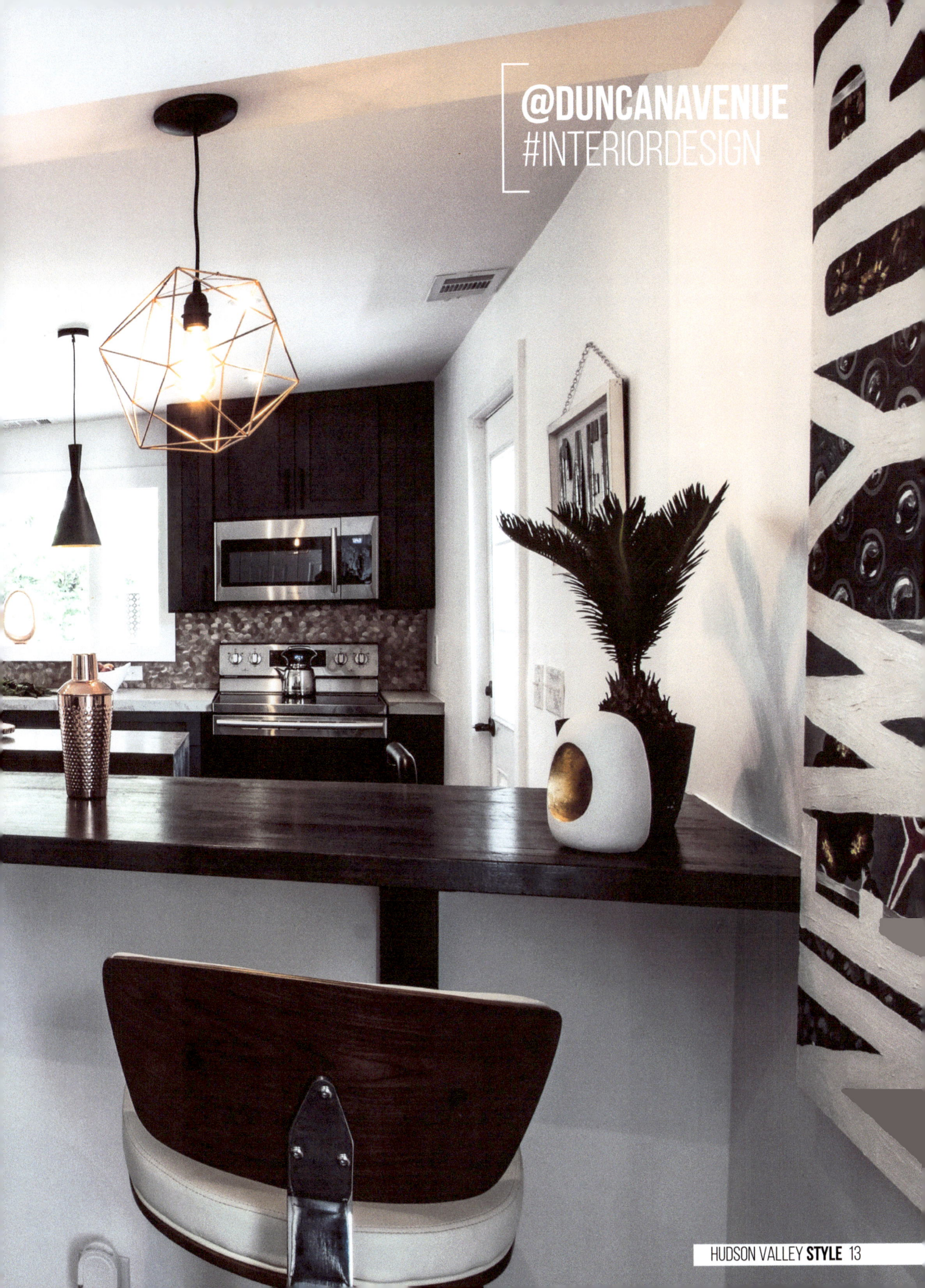

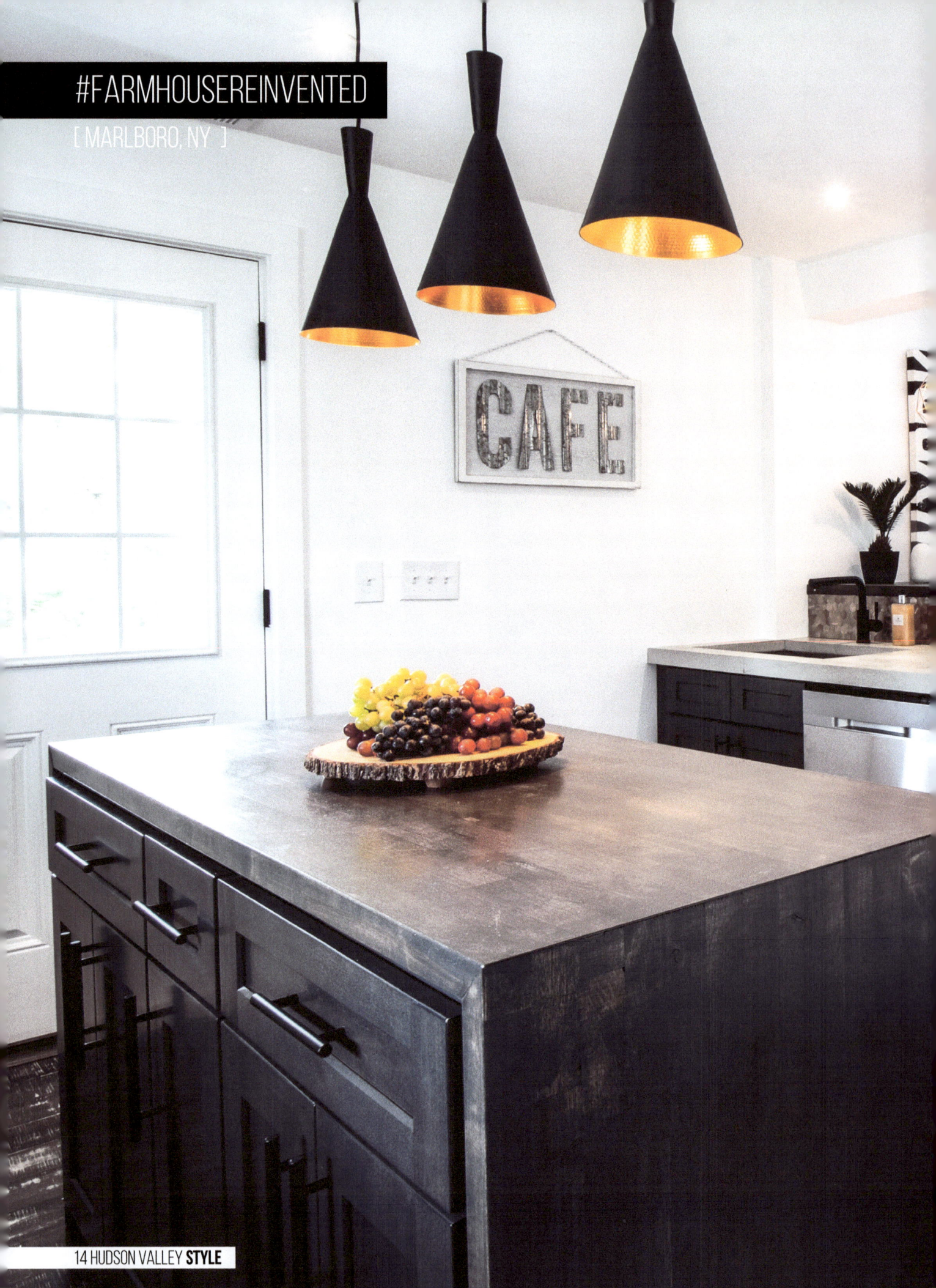

CONTEMPORARY SMART FLOOR PLAN

Contemporary open concept floorplan, glass french doors and 210° wraparound porch with 3-season outdoor dining space blur the line between indoor and outdoor living and allow residents and guests to enjoy a true connection with surrounding nature.

Wake up to the sunrise shining through double glass doors on the east side of the house and watch the warm sunset rays shining through plenty of energy-efficient windows and french doors on the west. High-end finishes such as sustainable bamboo hardwood floors, sustainable concrete countertops, solid wood kitchen cabinets with soft closing drawers, energy star stainless steel appliances, and designer light fixtures are only a few of the updates along with a brand-new central HVAC heat pump system controlled by smart Nest thermostat with two-zone sensors.

Brand new roof, utilities, and all LED lighting bring additional value and comfort for many years to come. The property features a beautiful designer pergola on the edge of the hill with an opportunity for the in-ground infinity pool. Property's sun number is 91 and is all set for installation of your own solar farm that will take the property go 100% off-grid.

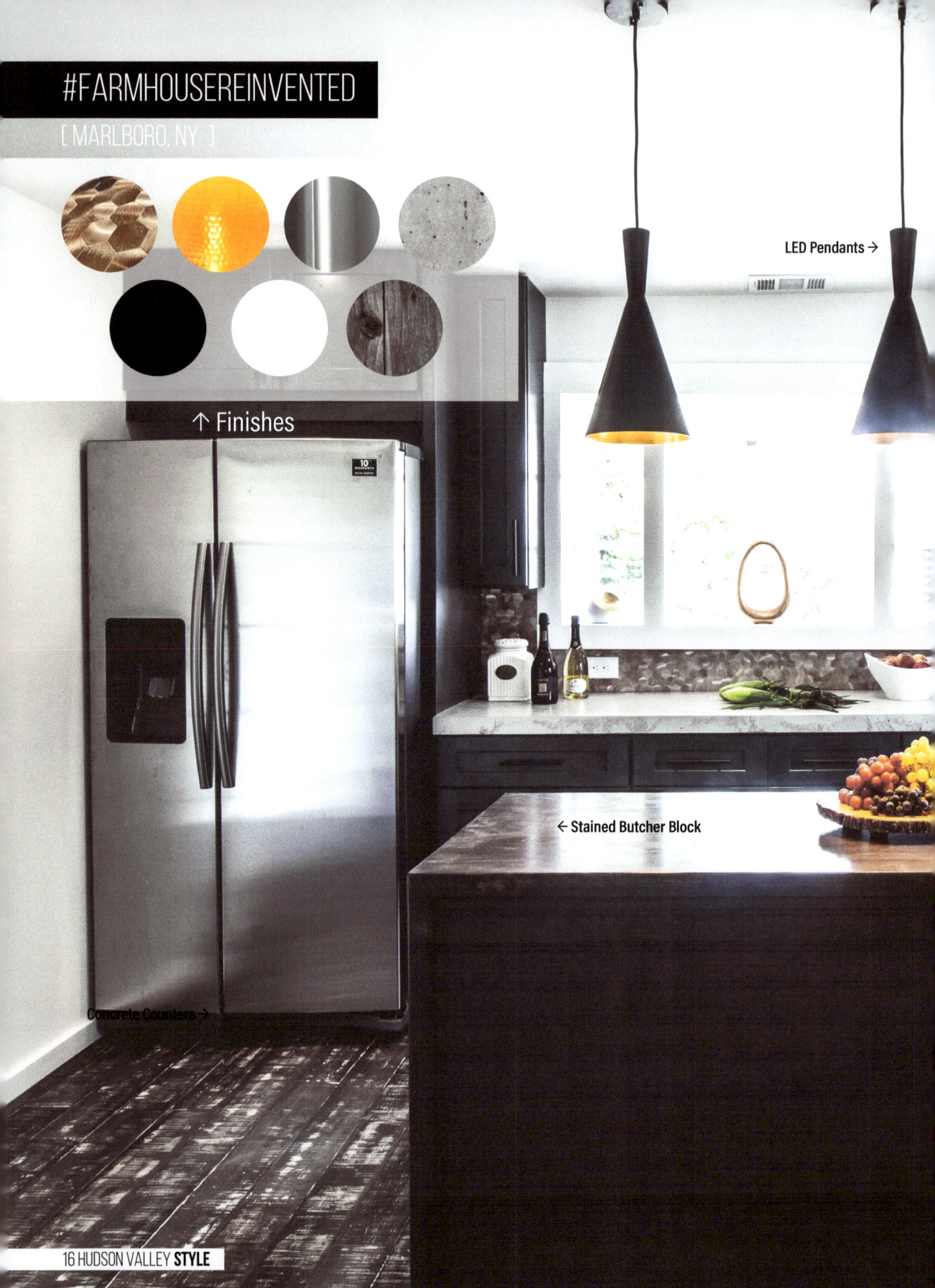

#FARMHOUSEREINVENTED
[MARLBORO, NY]

↑ Finishes

LED Pendants →

← Stained Butcher Block

Concrete Counters →

16 HUDSON VALLEY STYLE

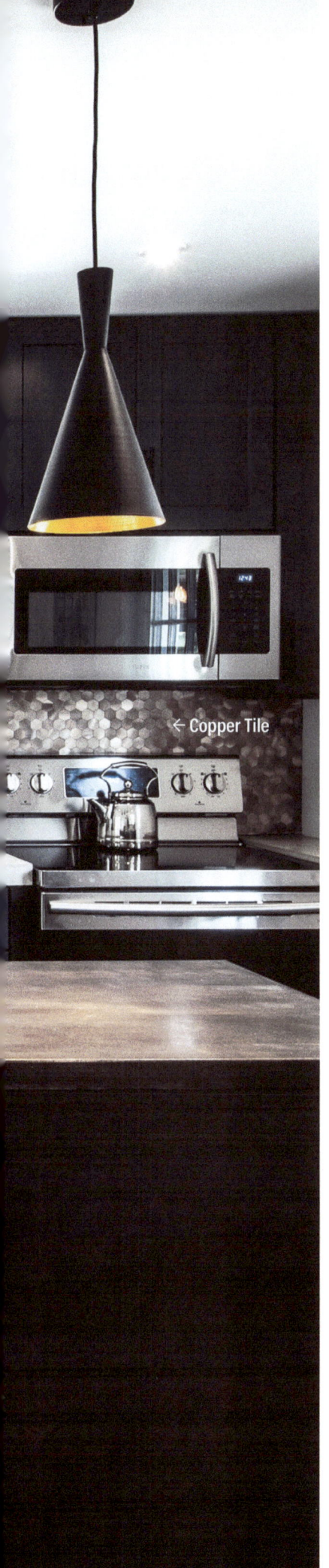

← Copper Tile

SUSTAINABLE CONCRETE & WOOD COUNTERTOPS

This kitchen has a lot of character thanks to the sophisticated/industrial look of concrete countertops. They are not just trendy, but also environmentally-friendly. One of the unique characteristics of concrete is that this material will evolve and adopt character over time, so the appearance of your counters will improve with age. Concrete counters are durable and heat-resistant for all of you avid bakers out there. The material is non-toxic, does not emit VOCs unlike plastics/polymers and is a sustainable material, unlike granite or marble. Concrete is a friend of the environment in all stages of its life span, from raw material production to demolition, making it a natural choice for sustainable home construction.

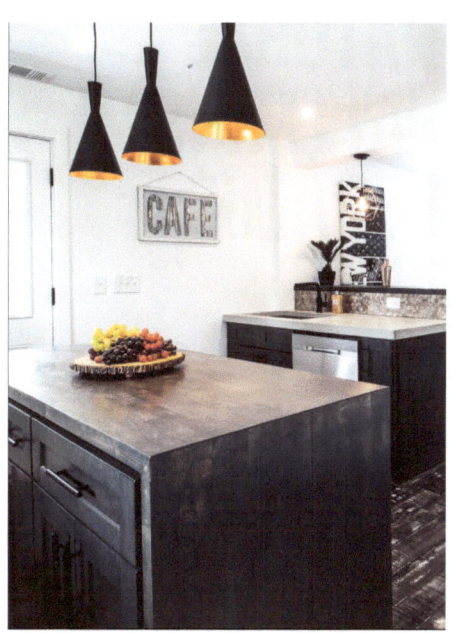

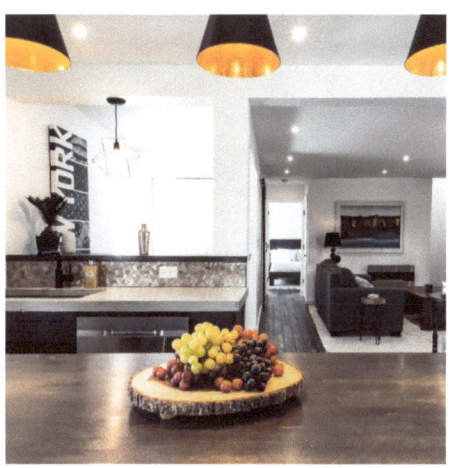

STAINLESS STEEL ENERGY STAR APPLIANCES

Stainless Steel Energy Star Appliances are an important accord in an overall symphony of this amazing and functional kitchen. They are positioned in the most efficient way to ensure an easy cooking process. The kitchen features range hood vented outside of the house and stylish yet environmentally-friendly electric range. Hudson Valley region energy providers offer an option to switch to 100% renewable electricity from wind and solar, so the electric range makes a lot of sense.

#FARMHOUSEREINVENTED
[MARLBORO, NY]

NATURAL PATTERNS CERAMIC TILE MATTE BLACK ACCENTS

Natural look and natural materials. This time we went with darker accents colors, but overall both bathrooms in this house are bright and airy.

FLOATING VANITIES & BARN DOORS, CERAMIC TILE, DESIGNER LED LIGHT FIXTURES, AN ABUNDANCE OF LIGHT & SPACE CREATE AN INSPIRING SPA-LIKE EXPERIENCE

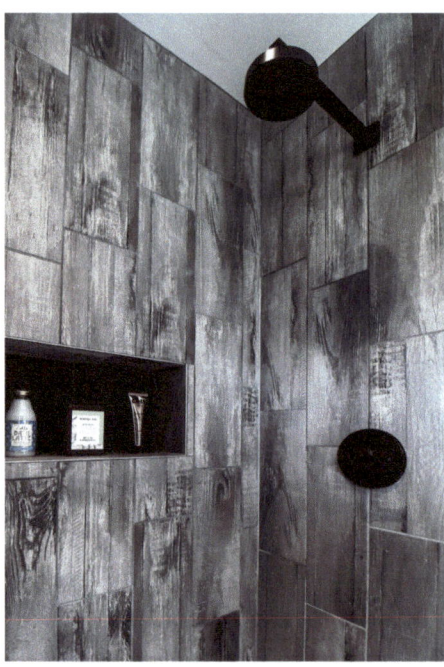

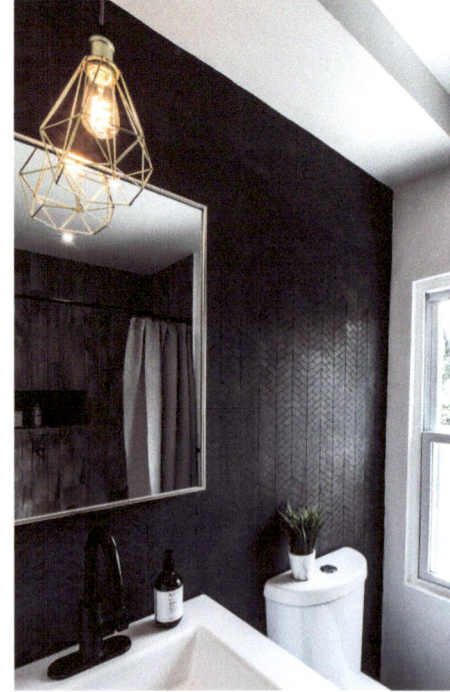

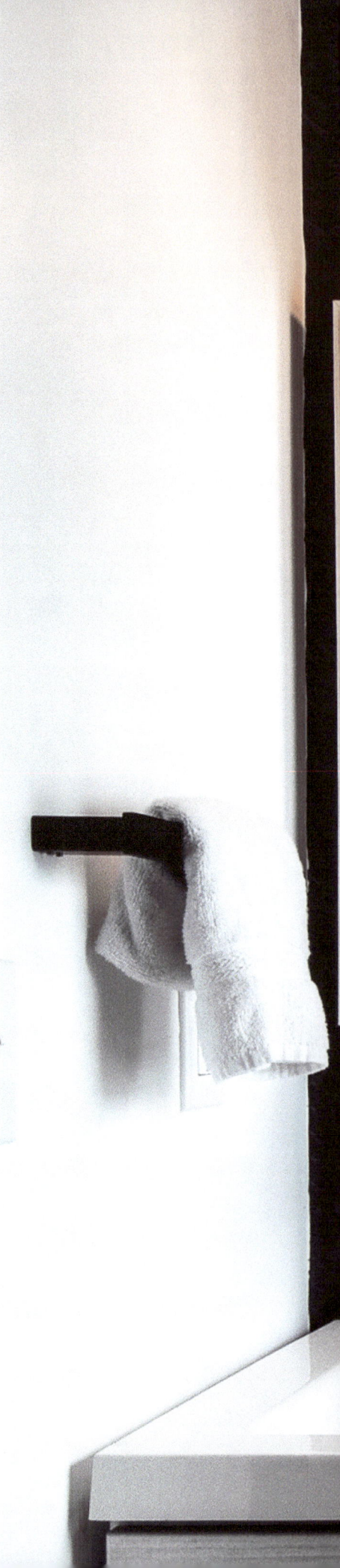

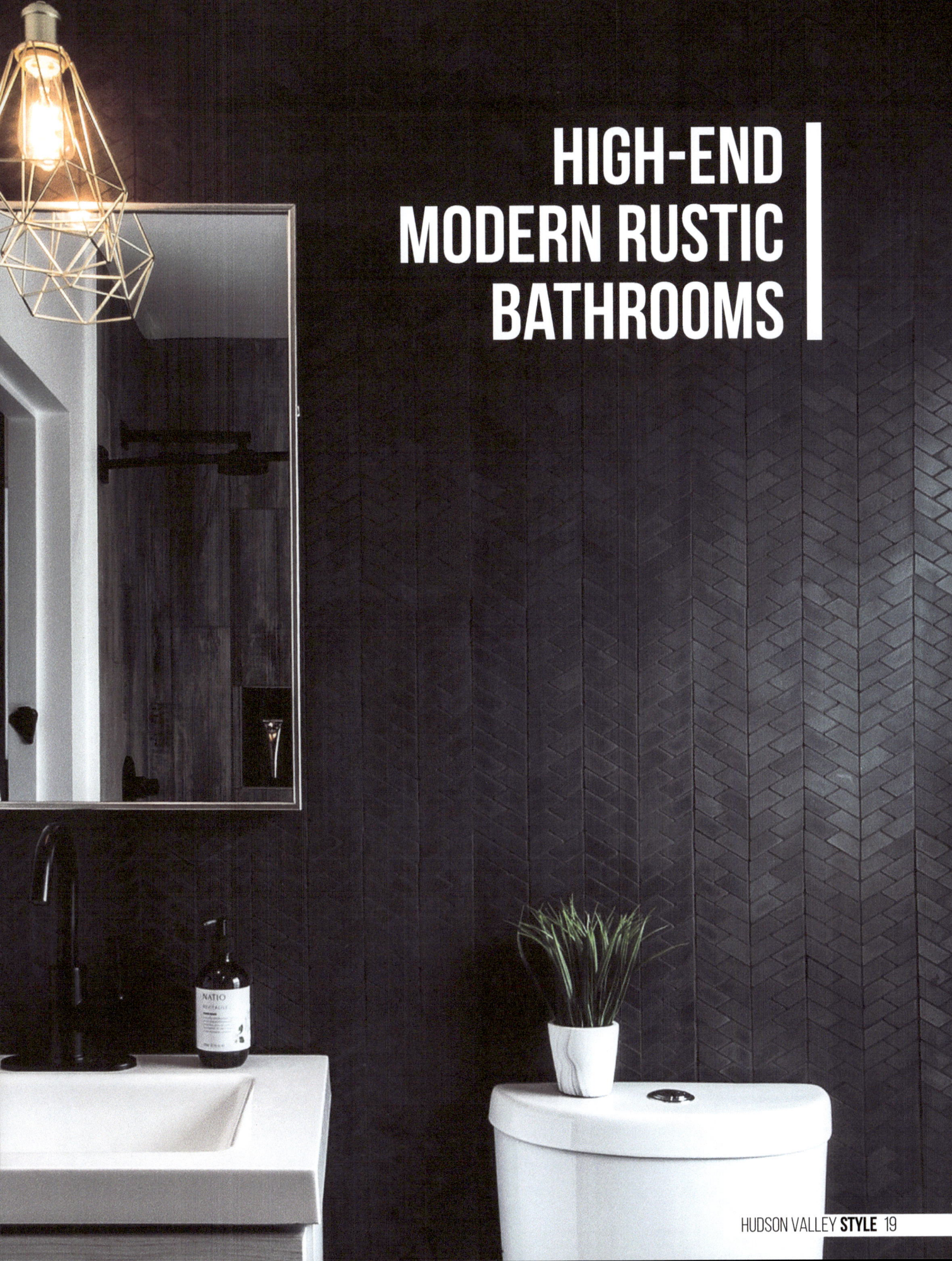
HIGH-END MODERN RUSTIC BATHROOMS

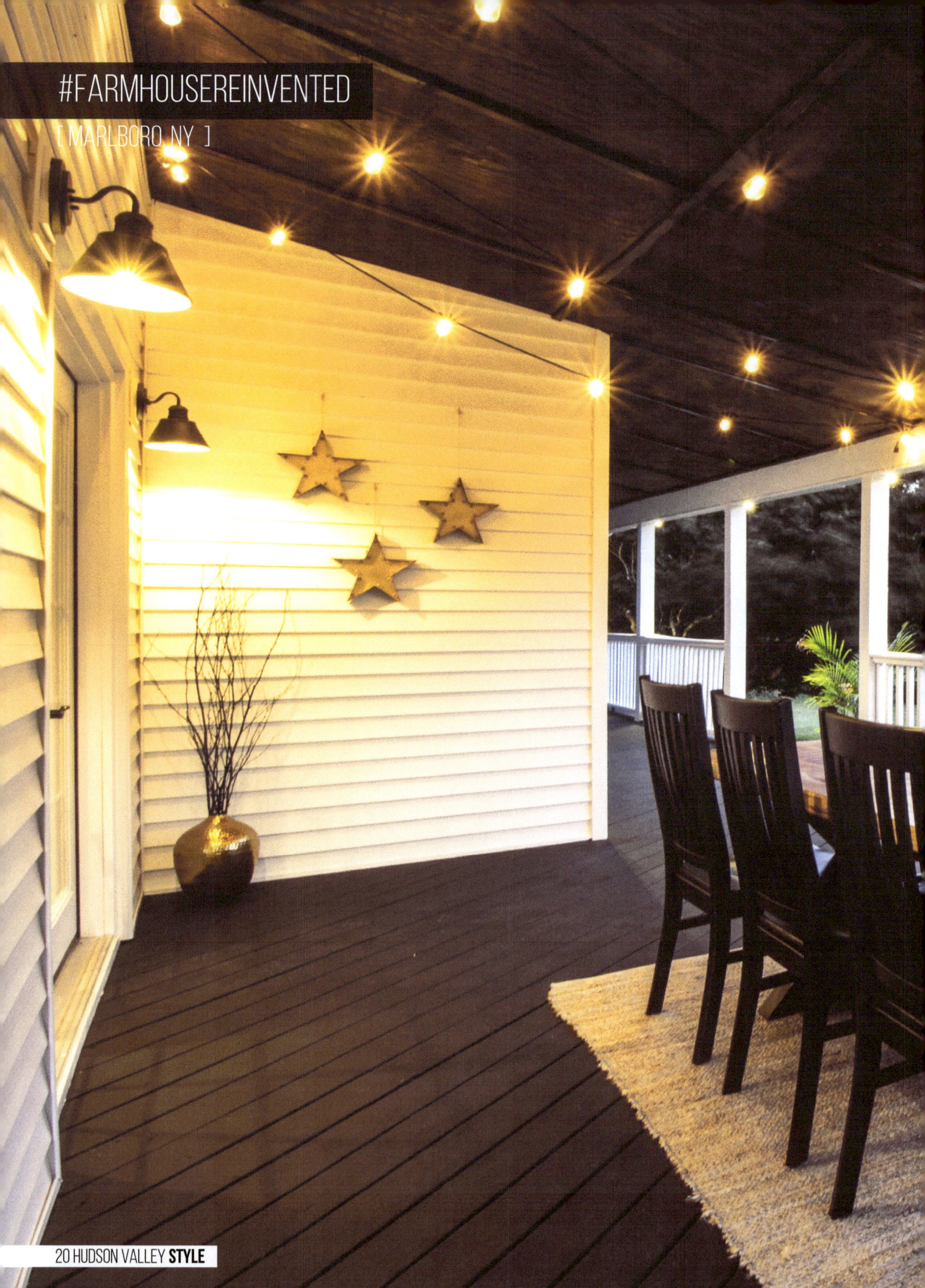

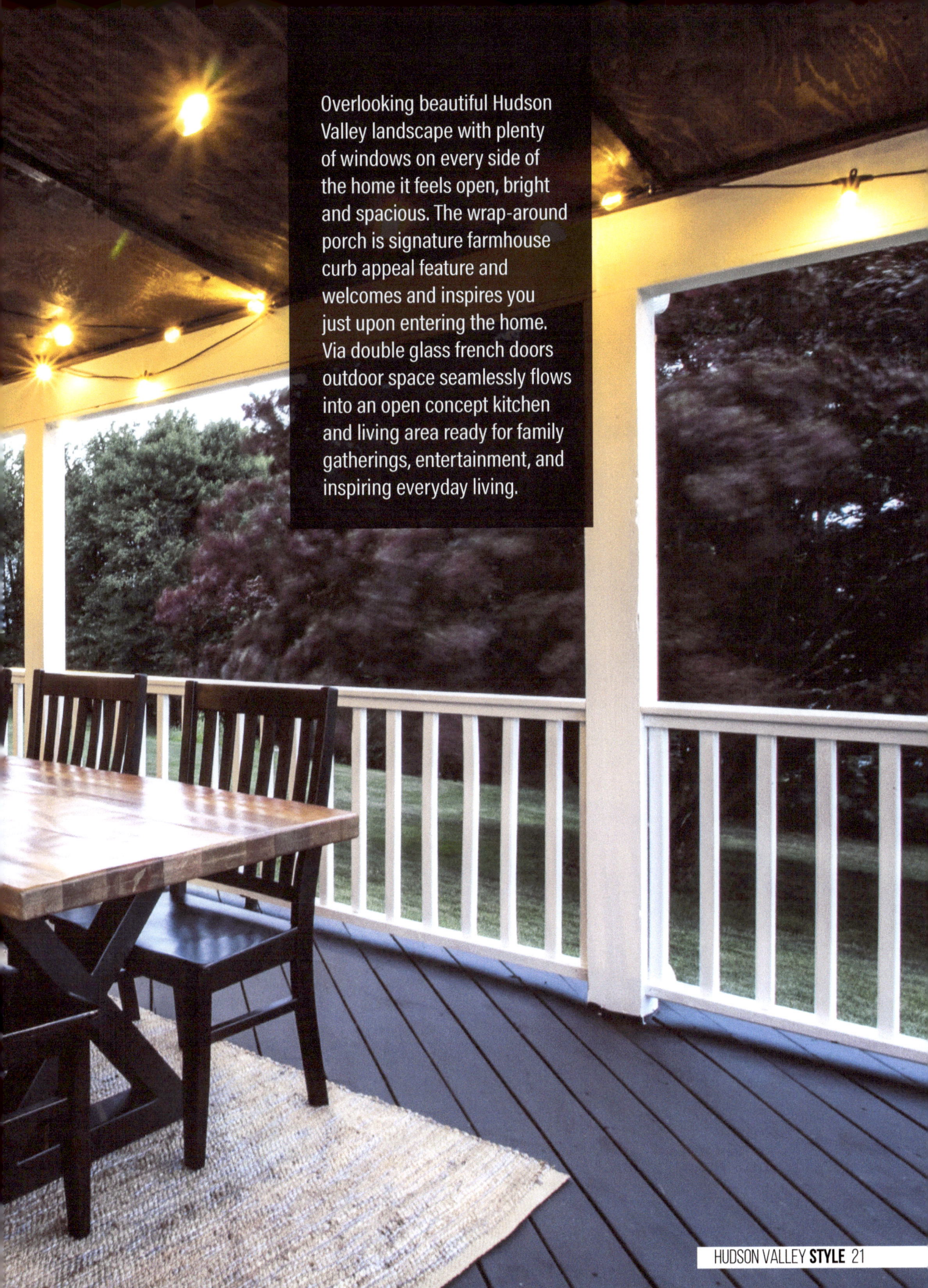

Overlooking beautiful Hudson Valley landscape with plenty of windows on every side of the home it feels open, bright and spacious. The wrap-around porch is signature farmhouse curb appeal feature and welcomes and inspires you just upon entering the home. Via double glass french doors outdoor space seamlessly flows into an open concept kitchen and living area ready for family gatherings, entertainment, and inspiring everyday living.

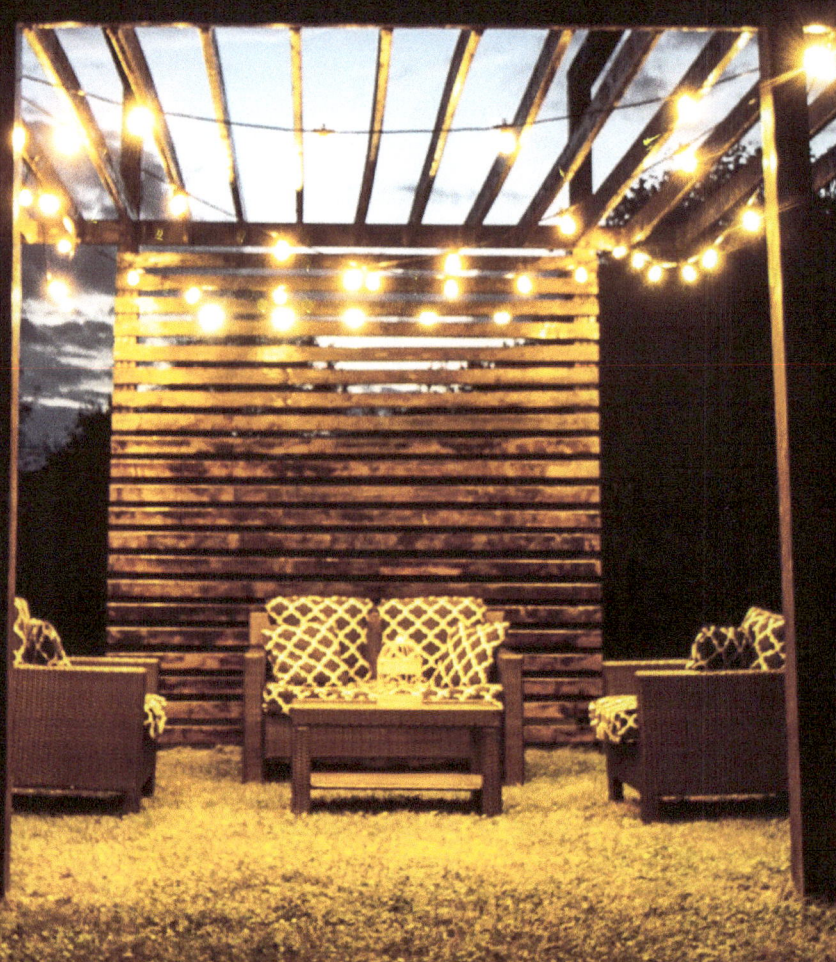

#FARMHOUSEREINVENTED
[MARLBORO, NY]

OUTDOOR LIVING

[LEARN MORE ABOUT THIS AND OTHER INTERIOR DESIGN/RENOVATION PROJECTS AT
DUNCANAVENUE.COM

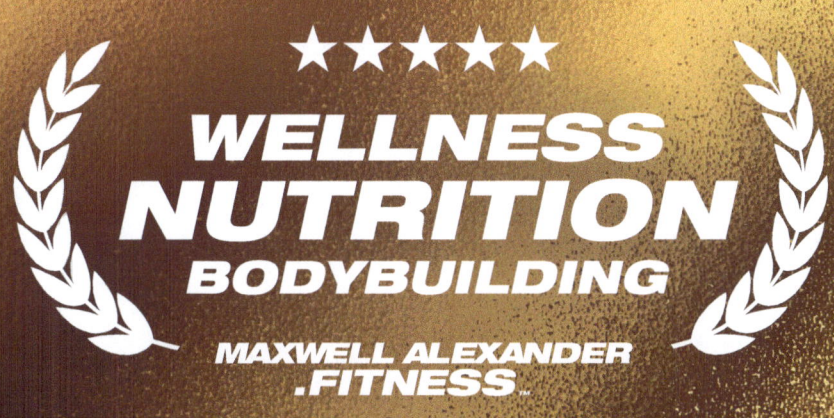

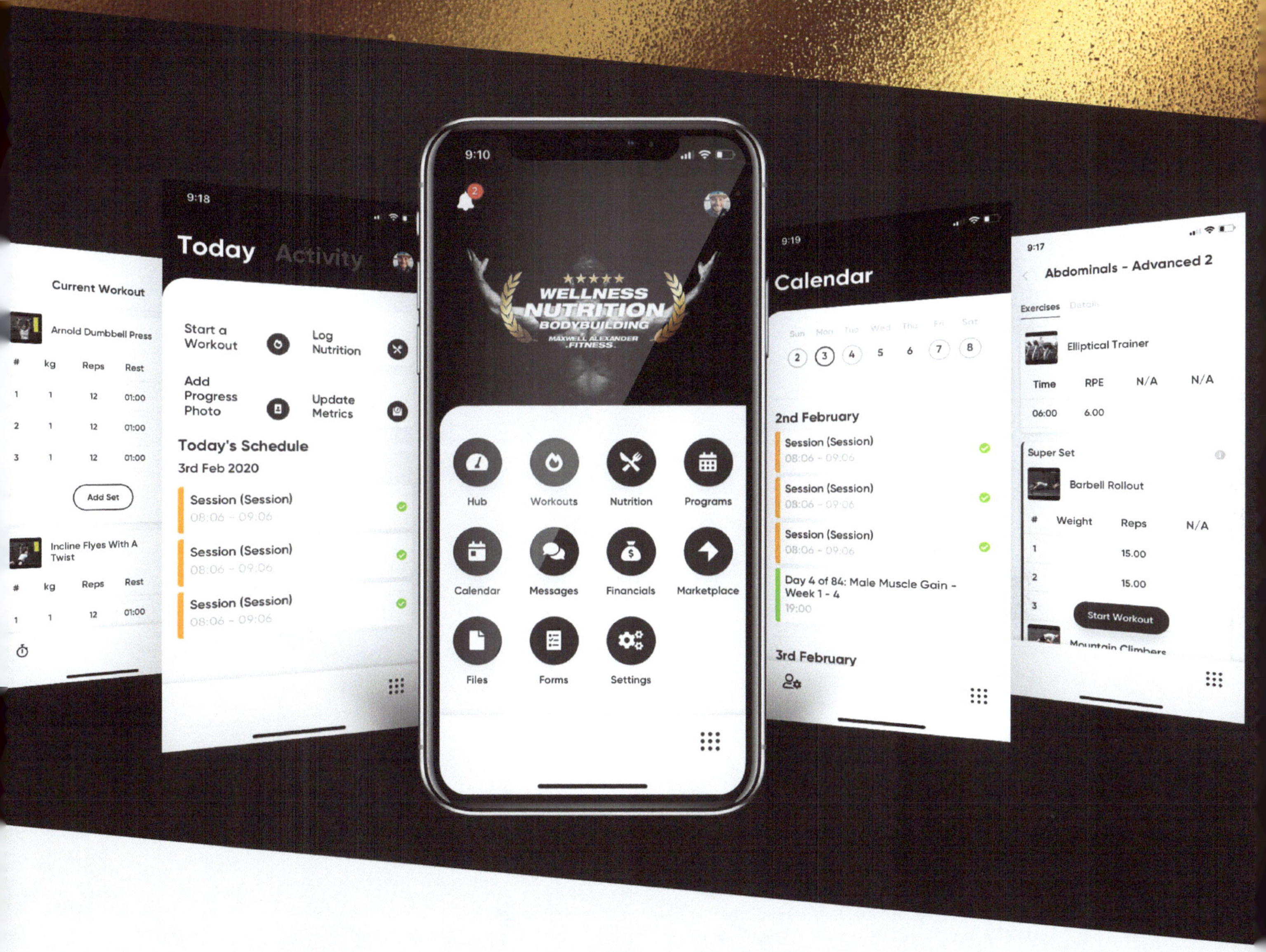

BRANDING HUDSON VALLEY REAL ESTATE FOR THE GLOBAL MARKET

**BY DINO ALEXANDER
CEO, ALEXANDER MAXWELL REALTY**

In today's market, real estate investors, as well as regular buyers are spoilt for choice. Even the best location is no longer enough when it comes to competing on a Global Market and this is when Strategic Branding comes into play. Luxury Real Estate Properties do not sell overnight and require a long-term Brand Strategy.

By definition, brand strategy is a long-term plan for the development of a successful brand in order to achieve specific goals. A well-defined and executed brand strategy affects all aspects of a business and is directly connected to consumer needs, emotions, and competitive environments. In real estate stakes are much higher just because the subject of the branding process is a single product and the goal is one transaction - property sale.

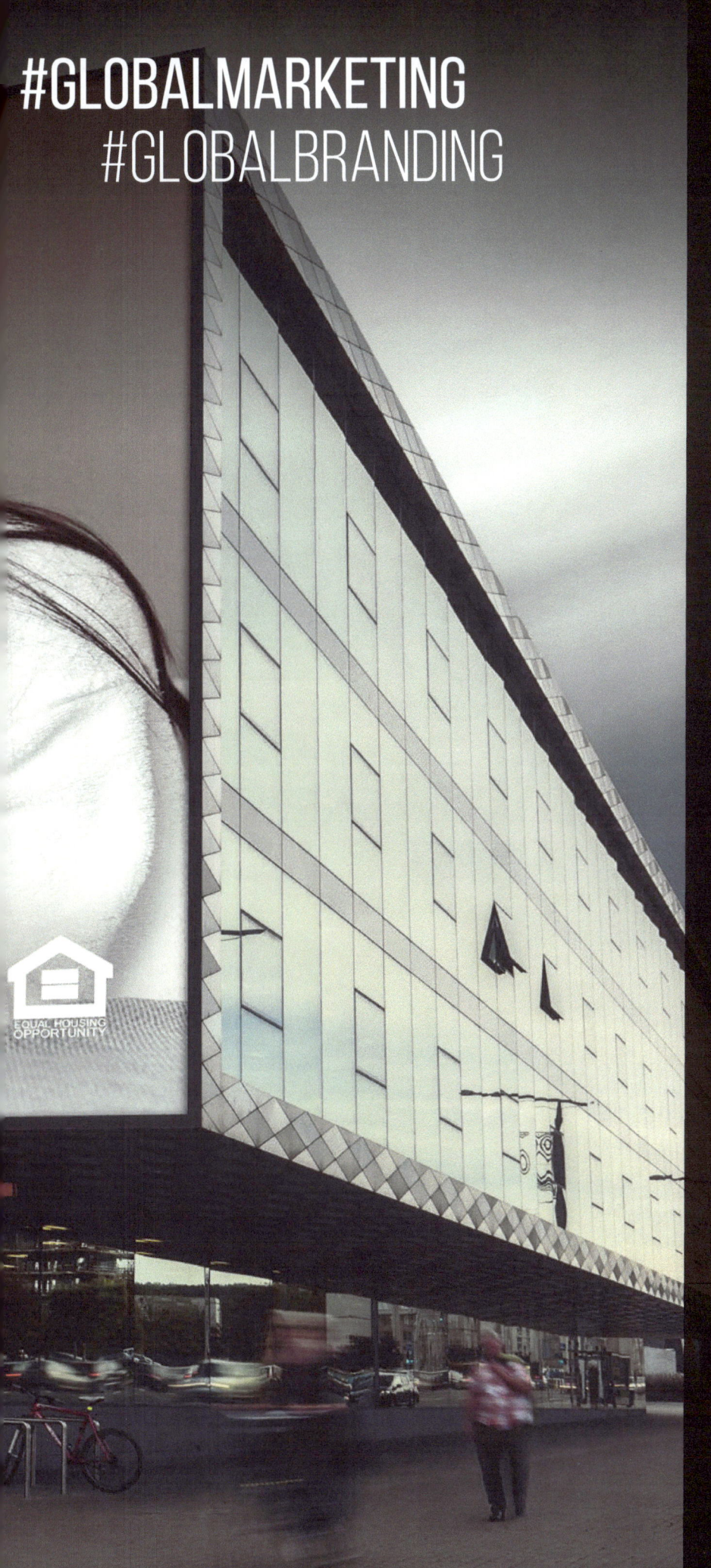

#GLOBALMARKETING
#GLOBALBRANDING

A WELL-DEFINED AND EXECUTED BRAND STRATEGY AFFECTS ALL ASPECTS OF A BUSINESS & IS DIRECTLY CONNECTED TO CONSUMER NEEDS, EMOTIONS, & COMPETITIVE ENVIRONMENTS

Alexander Maxwell Realty has partnered with award-winning Duncan Avenue Studio and together has more than a decade of experience branding products and services competing on the Global Market. Our clients include world-renown global economy players, Fortune 500 Companies, technology startups, wellness, and fitness brands, medical, manufacturing, real estate brands, NGOs as well as government agencies. Each property listed with Alexander Maxwell Realty becomes a unique World-Class Brand and presented to the local and global audience of real estate buyers through our high-end PR and marketing channels.

Logon to almaxrealty.com to schedule your listing consultation.

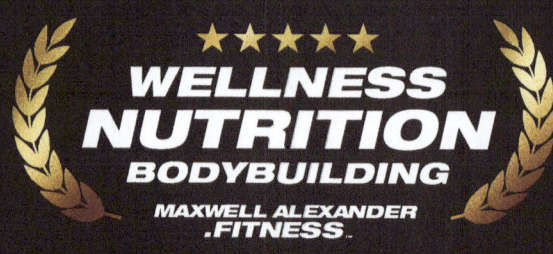

**WELLNESS
NUTRITION
BODYBUILDING**

MAXWELL ALEXANDER
.FITNESS

LIVE A LIFE OF VICTORY

Log On to MaxwellAlexander.Fitness
to **Start Your Transformation
Journey TODAY!**

[KITCHEN DESIGN TRENDS]

DESIGN YOUR KITCHEN LIKE A MILLENNIAL

by **Maxwell Alexander**

[KITCHEN DESIGN TRENDS]

Ah, Millennials, it warms my heart writing about Us – the most consciously awaken generation humans produced so far. We literally design the world around us in sync with Nature and the Universe. So what does it means to design a kitchen like a Millennial?

KITCHEN IS THE NEW LIVING ROOM

Millennials are awakening to the wisdom of the Cosmic Intelligence and taking into account the experience of the previous generations, they realize that anything related to food is crucial to our existence, not only because of the physical nourishment and wellbeing but also as a spiritual connection with our innate nature and other human beings. Sitting around a fire pit while preparing and sharing food, socializing, creating stories and memories is where life happened for our ancestors who were a lot closely connected to Nature. Millennials spend a great deal of their time not only socializing, but also working in coffee shops recreating the ancient environment and conditions where humans operate most efficiently while feeling their best. Now that Millennials are finally ready to build their own nests, and knowing that they will spend most of their time with the family cooking organic meals and socializing in the fully equipped kitchen, they bring the coffee shop concept with them. Walls are crumbling, dining rooms are being torn down – Millenials are hard at work making the open floor plan a reality.

Whew! The era of plastics is officially over! Thank you, but no thank you, Babyboomers! We are back to basics and embracing wood, steel, concrete, and natural stone. Walls, floors, furniture, and appliances are things we touch and in the air, we breathe, so why should it emit toxic fumes in the space where we spend most of our time? Plus, the use of sustainable materials like wood proactively protects the climate and serves as a repository of carbon emissions. Millennials are ditching their mom's plastic countertops and replacing them with simple, environmentally-friendly and cost-efficient concrete or quartz counters.

Millennial way or not, it's a great time to rethink your kitchen design. **Duncan Avenue Design Studio** is Hudson Valley's leading interior design agency and in collaboration with **Tough Construct | Hudson Valley**, they can execute a jaw-dropping overhaul of your kitchen space.

Visit ToughConstruct.com to learn more.

What you won't find in the Millennial's kitchen/living/dining space is a TV. Fortunately, Millennials hadn't had a chance to get hooked on the whole "cable" idea, whatever entertainment they need to get is at everyone's fingertips, so there is no reason to cover all the beautiful natural concrete/stucco walls with obnoxious plastic panels. In the meantime, a chalkboard is a great alternative to digital overload, so why not make an entire wall as a billboard for family-wide announcements, recipe display or a point of creative collaboration!

MILLENNIALS ARE BACK TO BASICS WHEN IT COMES TO CHOOSING INTERIOR MATERIALS

[KITCHEN DESIGN TRENDS]

INDUSTRIAL AUTHENTIC RUSTIC

CLASSY INDUSTRIAL LOOK, MODERN RUSTIC STYLE

Modern Rustic, Industrial Style is hot, especially with Millennials who appreciate reusing and recycling while staying classy and sophisticated. If you squint your eyes in Millennial's kitchen, you'll see a lot of grey-ish, brown-ish, black-ish and whitish colors reflecting in natural light. Remember the caves we lived in generations ago? I bet you'd see the same picture if you squint your eyes in one of those. Industrial shelving solutions are so in and you still got a chance to find a great deal at a nearby scrap metal place or a flea market. Hit garage sales this weekend for unique and environmentally conscious furniture. Dig into your grandma's attic for one of a kind decor for your Millennials-inspired kitchen.

FENG SHUI, YING YANG, BALANCE...

Wellness is about balance and Millennials take both very seriously. Whether you are a fan of centuries-old feng shui traditions, understand why Ying can't survive without Yang, or just following a common sense and balanced approach, you'd know that too much of good could be just as bad. Balance is the key, especially in kitchen design. Space should flow naturally, with enough square footage to breathe. Entrance to the kitchen should be either wide or cleared of any obstructions. Having storage in the kitchen is essential, however, try to hide unappealing items in cabinets below eye level and balance shelving with clear wall space ("white space" in layout design). If you use feng shui practice to decorate your home, you know the power of plants. Plants attract good energy. They also absorb negative energy and distractions. Surround yourself, neatly, with large smooth-leaved plants in earthenware pots. The plants and pottery represent the mountains and create supportive energy. Two good plant choices are the golden pothos and areca palm.

SCIENTIFICALLY JUSTIFIED & CULTURALLY EMBRACED SMART LIGHTING DESIGN

Lighting is a crucial element in interior design and if you are spending most of your time in your kitchen/living/dining/socializing space, you should know the facts. Lighting is like a lens that reveals the reality around us, and if the lens has an incorrect prescription, it will sure to give you a headache and affect your health negatively. Millennials are the smartest generation in the history of human civilization, they dictate the new lighting design trends:

An abundance of natural light is the best way to go. Our bodies are designed to thrive in the natural light, so it's important to welcome it inside the kitchen space.
LED Edison bulbs use a lot less energy and generate warmer light frequencies that create a cozy and stress-free ambiance.
Oversized industrial light fixtures are trendy and great at preventing the artificial light sources shine directly into your eyes and guide the light rays where they are needed.

WHO IS YOUR BUYER?

[MILLENNIALS]

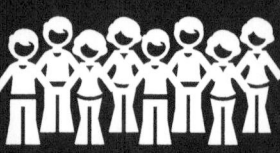 **36%**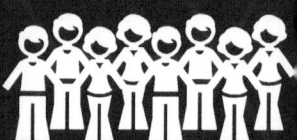
[THE LARGEST MARKET SHARE]

 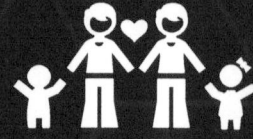 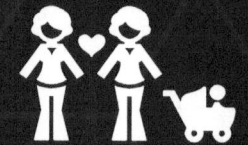 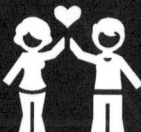

65% — FIRST-TIME HOME BUYERS
48% — HAVE CHILDREN
66% — MARRIED COUPLES
15% — UNMARRIED COUPLES

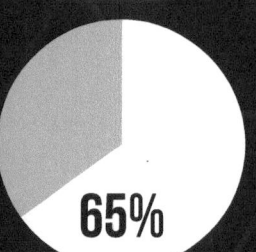 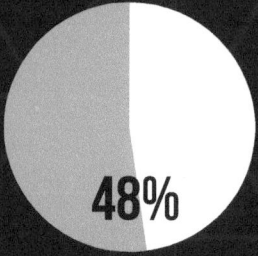 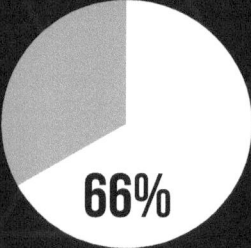 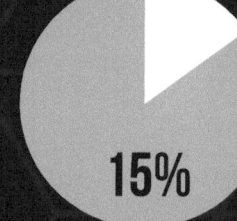

GENERATION X — 38-52 Y/O

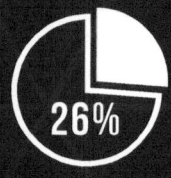 **26%** [OF ALL HOMEBUYERS]

$104,700 [MEDIAN INCOME]

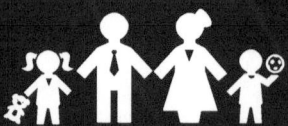 MOST LIKELY TO BE MARRIED & MOST LIKELY TO HAVE CHILDREN

[MOST RACIALLY & ETHNICALLY DIVERSE]
26% IDENTIFYING THEY ARE A RACE OTHER THAN WHITE/CAUCASIAN

BUY THE LARGEST HOMES IN MEDIAN SQFT.
PURCHASE THE HIGHEST MEDIAN PRICED HOMES

[YOUNGER BABY BOOMERS]
53-62 Y/O
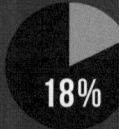 **18%**

[OLDER BABY BOOMERS]
63-71 Y/O
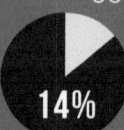 **14%**

[THE SILENT GENERATION]
72-92 Y/O
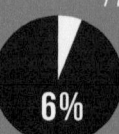 **6%**

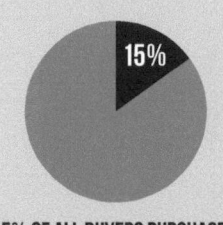
15% OF ALL BUYERS PURCHASED NEW CONSTRUCTION

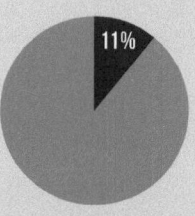
11% OF MILLENNIALS PURCHASED NEW CONSTRUCTION

85% PURCHASED PREVIOUSLY OWNED HOMES
[MILLENNIALS: 89%]

MOST IMPORTANT **ENVIRONMENTAL FEATURES:**
HEATING & COOLING COSTS

TYPICAL HOME RECENTLY PURCHASED
1,870 SQFT.
3 BDRM.
2 BATH.

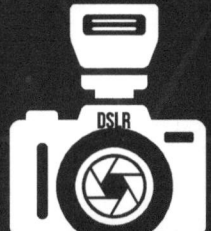

90%

"**90% OF BUYERS** UNDER AGE OF 62 CONSIDER **PHOTOGRAPHY** AS THE MOST IMPORTANT FEATURE WHEN SEARCHING ONLINE"

DATA SOURCE: 2018 HOME BUYER AND SELLER GENERATIONAL TRENDS REPORT BY THE NATIONAL ASSOCIATION OF REALTORS®

almaxrealty ™
[ALEXANDER MAXWELL REALTY]

SELLING YOUR PROPERTY?
ASK US ABOUT **COMPLIMENTARY** ALL-INCLUSIVE
STRATEGIC MARKETING PACKAGE

LOG ON TO **ALMAXREALTY.COM** & JOIN US ON INSTAGRAM! **@ALMAXREALTY**

[PRESENTED BY ALMAXREALTY.COM]

[HUDSON VALLEY STYLE TREND]

2020 INTERIOR DESIGN TREND: BARN DOORS

Barn doors are no longer an outdoor feature, but a stylish yet rustic Hudson Valley Style interior design trend. Known for their functionality and space-saving features, they are in high demand among ToughConstruct clients in Hudson Valley's Cornwall on Hudson, New Windsor, Newburgh, Wallkill, Goshen, Pine Bush, and Beacon areas. With the help of ToughConstruct (2018 Hudson Valley Style, Design & Sustainability Awards Winner), discover why adding a barn door is an ideal home improvement project that will bring modern rustic style into your home.

BARN DOORS ARE A PERFECT ELEMENT TO CONNECT ROOMS WITHIN AN OPEN FLOORPLAN

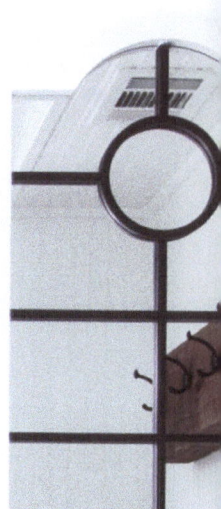

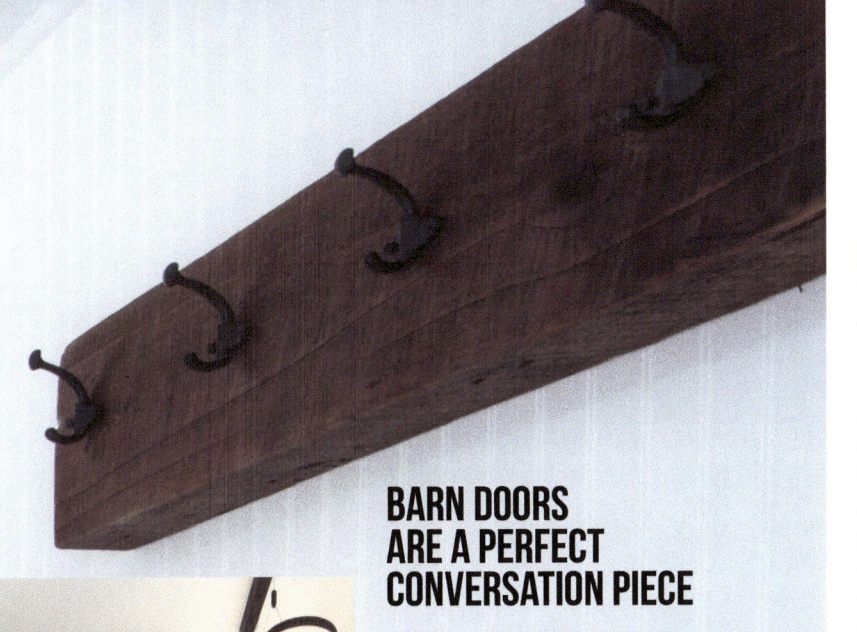

BARN DOORS ARE A PERFECT CONVERSATION PIECE

Interior doors are not just art hanging on the wall, but also serves an important function, they also can showcase a homeowner's style and personality. Barn doors are a perfect conversation piece when entertaining family and friends. If your home is lacking a statement piece that inspires creativity and sparks conversation, contact ToughConstruct today to get a free quote for a custom-built barn door that will perfectly fit your space. Take a look at brand door examples of ToughConstruct's previous clients.

CUSTOM BARN DOORS ARE TRENDY YET CLASSY

Just like a piece of clothing, home decor often goes out of style, however, barn doors have been around for centuries and are an essential part of the Authentic Hudson Valley Style. Many Hudson Valley homeowners go with a modern, sophisticated look, rustic wood look or with a chalkboard barn door that adds another layer of functionality in the kitchen or a kid's room.

Adding a custom-built barn door in your Hudson Valley home could dramatically

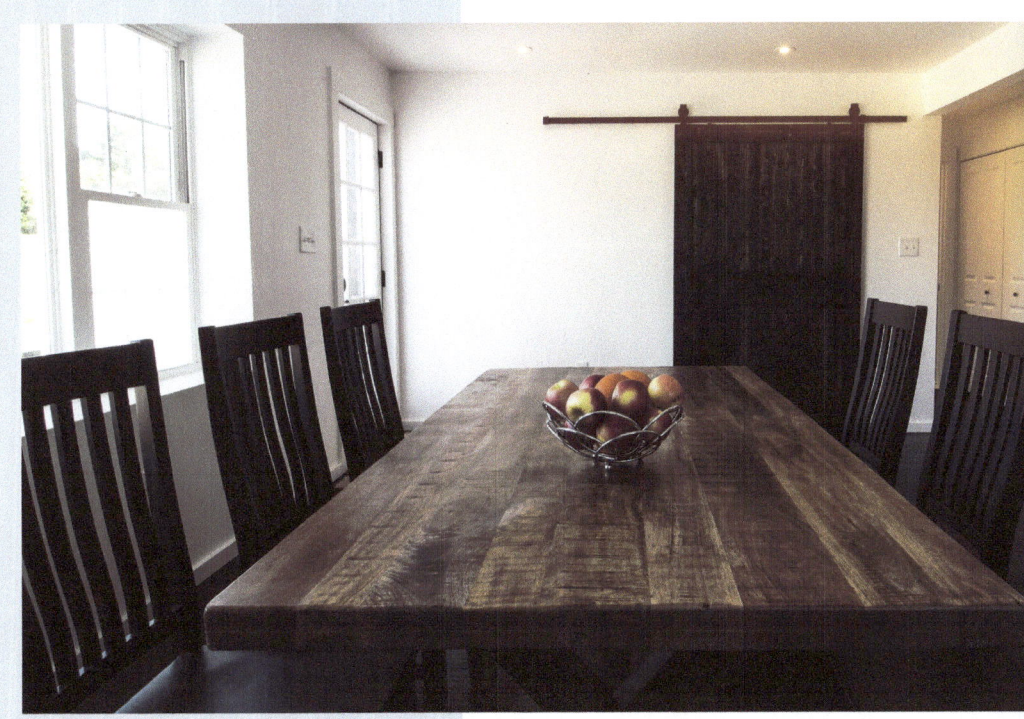

As open floor plans gain popularity among homeowners in the greater Hudson Valley region, interior doors are evolving as well. Barn doors are one of the most efficient yet trendy approaches to connect adjacent rooms into one open floorplan space.

"The organic modern rustic look of custom barn doors adds warmth and cosy feeling into an interior," says Designer Maxwell Alexander of Duncan Avenue Design Studio. "The space-saving flexibility of a barn door is an important function of adjusting and controlling interior environment to one's liking." Conventional hinge-mounted doors are out of fashion and take 2 times more space than a barn door that slides on a rolling track.

improve interior design of a space, not only from a visual perspective but also from a functional perspective. Imagine adding a few more square feet of space that doesn't have to overlap with a door rotating on hinges? High-quality, custom-built brand doors by Hudson Valley's best contractor will refresh your interiors and make you ready to meet one of the most beautiful seasons in the Hudson Valley!

FITNESS TRAINER
SOPHIA MARTELLY
#FITLIFE
IG: @SOPHIAMARTELLY.FIT

INTERVIEW & PHOTOGRAPHY
BY MAXWELL ALEXANDER

MAKEUP & STYLING BY
ANCOLIE MARTELLY
IG: @ANCOLIE_MARTELLY_BRIDAL

" THERE IS NO BOOK THAT GIVES YOU DIRECTIONS TO FIGURE OUT LIFE AND EVERYONE REACHES THEIR GOALS ON THEIR OWN TIMELINE..."

SOPHIA MARTELLY
COVER STORY

NO ONE IS GOING TO REACH YOUR GOALS FOR YOU!

Maxwell Alexander: Wow! Congrats on an amazing cover photoshoot, Sophia! I must say, natural beauty always rocks! Let's don't waste any time and get to your #FitLife cover story right away: What happened? How did you arrive at the decision to become a personal fitness trainer?

Sophia Martelly:
I went to college. I picked a random major. I wasted time and money. I had no idea what I wanted to do in life. I feel like many young people go through a phase of figuring out how to find themselves and their purpose in this crazy life. It seemed like everyone around me had it all figured out and had been on the track to their life goals and dreams. When I started to talk to others about how I was feeling the more I realized that so many people around me were in the exact same boat. There is no book that gives you directions to figure out life and everyone reaches their goals on their own timeline which can be considerably different than others around them. Don't let this get you discouraged.

I CAME TO A POINT WHERE I KNEW THAT A DREAM JOB WAS NOT GOING TO JUST BE MAGICALLY THROWN AT ME. YOU HAVE TO WORK FOR WHAT YOU WANT.

I asked myself – What do you like and want to do? What is something that makes you effortlessly happy? What are you good at? I only had one answer….GYM! After years of second-guessing myself, asking these questions is what really helped me arrive at the decision to become a personal trainer.

I have always been active and played sports growing up, but I would have to say my passion for fitness really sparked when I was working at the front desk of a gym part-time. There I met so many new friends and people who loved to work out. I started working out with them and really learned and loved the art of training. I learned so many new techniques and diverse effective exercises.

Health and fitness have always been the focus of my life and as cliché, as it sounds – I turned my passion into my career. I began training myself, friends and family. Then I started the certification process and started professionally training at my local gym, Mac Fitness. I really love motivating my clients and pushing them to help reach their health and fitness goals. It is so satisfying to help others see results in their own fitness journey. I love what I do!

Maxwell Alexander: OMG, I can relate to like 99% of what you just said! In my case, I arrived at the fitness destination through my passion for design, which we will mention a bit later. For now, what's your favorite thing about living and working in Kingston (the First Capital of New York)?

Sophia Martelly:
My favorite part about living in the Kingston area definitely has to be our natural surroundings! I live in such a beautiful part of the Hudson Valley. The gorgeous landscape has always been my favorite part of the area. I love to spend my free time outside. There are endless hiking trails, and so many outdoor activities. Even in the winter I love that I am so close to the mountains to snowboard, it's so much fun and a great workout as well!

" I WAS WORKING OUT AT LEAST 5 DAYS A WEEK FOR 2 HOURS EACH DAY. SOME CALL IT CRAZY, I CALL IT PASSION."

My favorite part about working in the Kingston area is the location and short distance to and from NYC. Many of my clients have moved up from the city and a lot of them are very inspiring. It is always cool to get different outlooks and perspectives and hear different people's stories. I meet a lot of cool and unique people!

Maxwell Alexander:
Talking about proximity to the Capital of the World: What is your personal style and what is your definition of Hudson Valley Style?

Sophia Martelly:
My personal style is sporty. I'm in gym clothes every day of the week. I love that brands are

making gym clothes that are functional yet non-frumpy. I like to feel confident, strong, and sexy while I'm in the gym.

My definition of Hudson Valley Style has a lot to do with the beautiful landscape we live in. It also has to do with the diversity and beauty of the people who live here. We are one with the scenery around us. As a result,

WE ARE ADVENTUROUS, FRIENDLY, EARTH

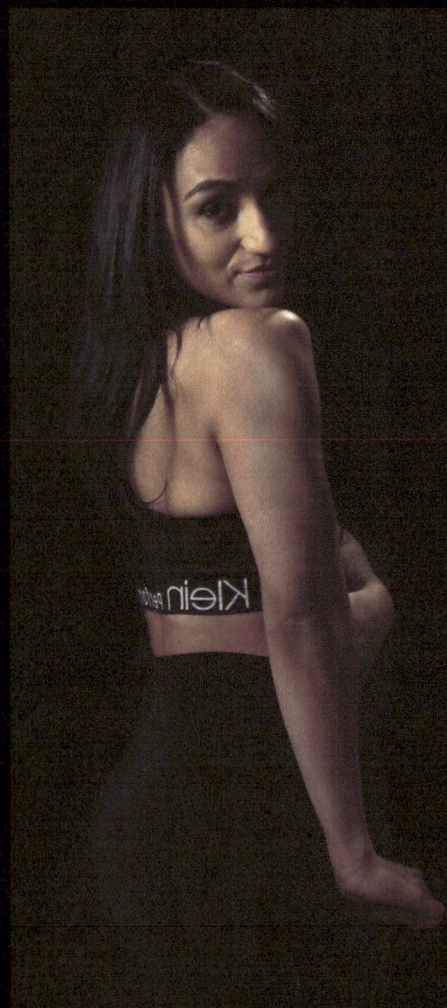

CONSCIOUS, AMBITIOUS, CREATIVE, AND MOST IMPORTANTLY, A COMMUNITY.

Maxwell Alexander:
There is so much talk about artificial intelligence lately and particularly how it helps us to design and build better bodies for humans (motorized body parts at the moment), but what about our natural human intelligence? Isn't what fitness trainers are doing since the age of the first Olympic games: creating better looking, stronger and more efficient human bodies? What's your take on this?

Sophia Martelly:
These days there is so much you can do to enhance your body. It seems like there is a technological solution for almost any ailment you may have. The problem is that these high-tech fixes focus on symptoms of the problem, not the cause. For the most part, you wouldn't need any "artificial intelligence" if you use your own logic and first prevent the problem through a daily healthy lifestyle, specifically your diet and fitness.

It's so funny how technology can be so complex yet the real solution and prevention is something so simple – daily exercise and a healthy diet.

You are the designer of your own life and you are the designer of your own body.

Your daily actions and lifestyle choices will be your results. If you are lazy and make excuses you will be unhappy and not see a positive change. If you take action and put forth the effort, your results will show and you will reach your goals.

SOME PEOPLE NEED A LITTLE MORE MOTIVATION & GUIDANCE THAN OTHERS

AND THAT IS WHERE HIRING A PERSONAL TRAINER WILL MAKE A HUGE DIFFERENCE.

I get that people want to be fit and healthy, but there is so much information out there it can be overwhelming and one might not know where to start. This is where my job comes into play. Not only do personal trainers help you create a better looking, stronger, and more efficient body, but at the same time, we are also providing you with better health, disease prevention, stress relief and a better quality of life. (Just to name a few benefits!)

The solution is simple. Choose wisely what food you use to fuel your body with and get up and move. People make time for what is important in their lives it's just all about what you are actually making a priority. You only get one body and you need to take care of it. Let me help you!

Maxwell Alexander:
And finally, what is your next big thing? Any hints on what we should expect from you in the near future?

Sophia Martelly:
It has always been a dream to incorporate my passion for the outdoors into my workouts. I would love to take clients hiking, biking, kayaking. We live in the beautiful Hudson Valley! Might as well take advantage of that. Taking this dream and making it a reality will be my next big thing. Not only are outdoor activities great for the body, but it's also so freeing to the mind.

Maxwell Alexander:
Awesome and thank you, Sophia! We are looking forward to seeing more of those positive vibes from you! Let's keep in touch and we'll definitely follow up with you soon on your hiking adventures!

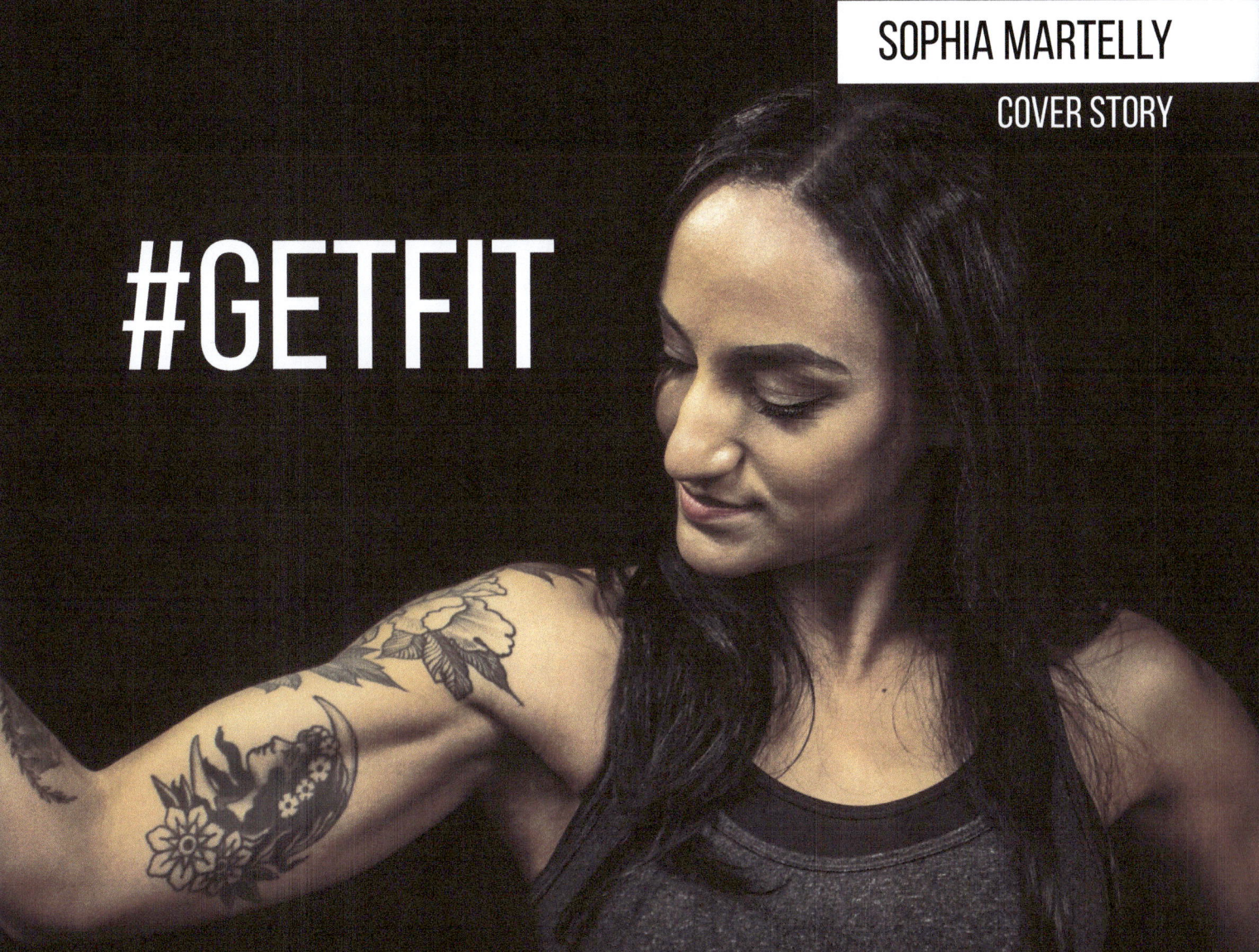

REAL ESTATE PHOTOGRAPHY 101

61% MORE VIEWS ONLINE WITH PROFESSIONAL PHOTOS

UP TO 47% HIGHER ASKING PRICE/SQFT

80% OF BUYERS CITED THEY WOULDN'T EVEN CONSIDER A LISTING WITHOUT PHOTOGRAPHS

98% OF BUYERS THINK PROFESSIONAL PHOTOS ARE MOST USEFUL WHEN LOOKING FOR HOME ONLINE

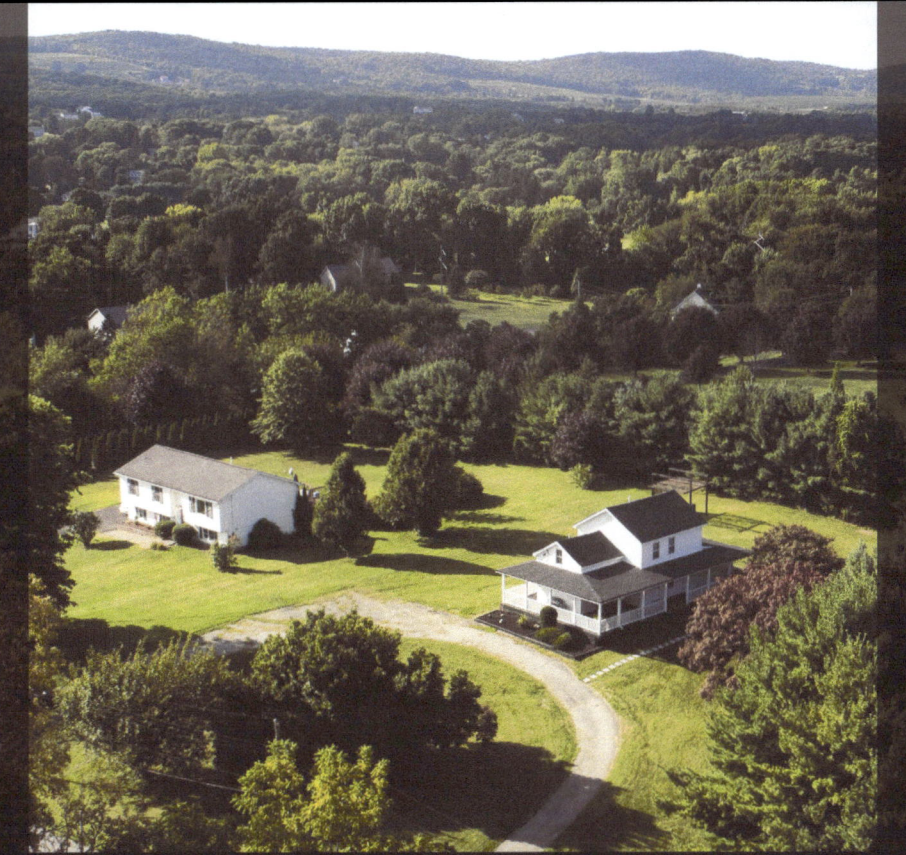
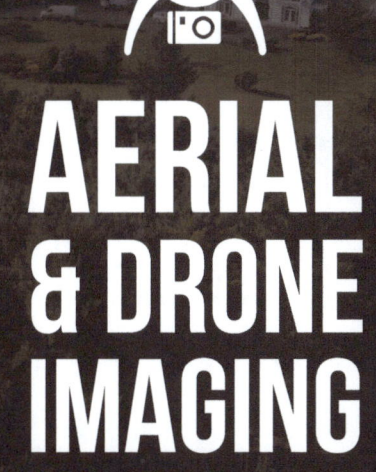

AERIAL & DRONE IMAGING

CONSIDER THESE HIGH-TECH UPGRADES

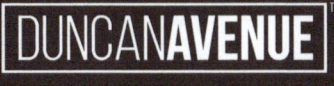
HUDSON VALLEY REAL ESTATE SERVICES

SCHEDULE YOUR PHOTOSHOOT @
DUNCANAVENUE.COM

STATISTICS SOURCE:
NATIONAL ASSOCIATION OF REALTORS

PROFESSIONAL LIGHTING
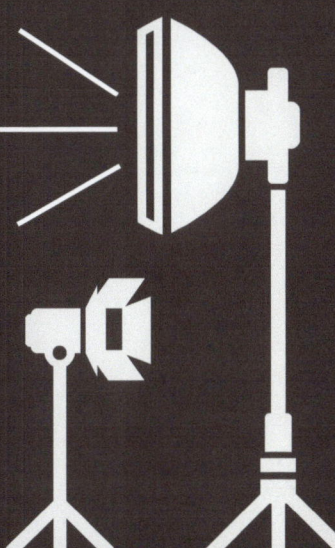

DSLR CAMERAS & LENSES
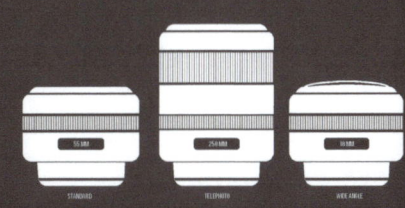
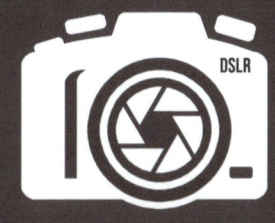

PROFESSIONAL RETOUCHING
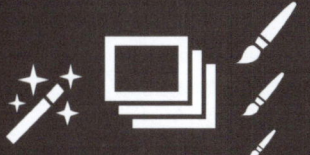

+ DIGITAL STAGING
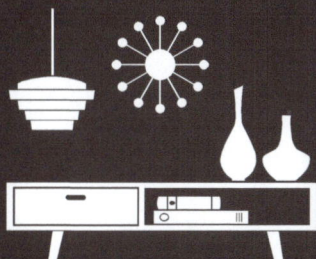

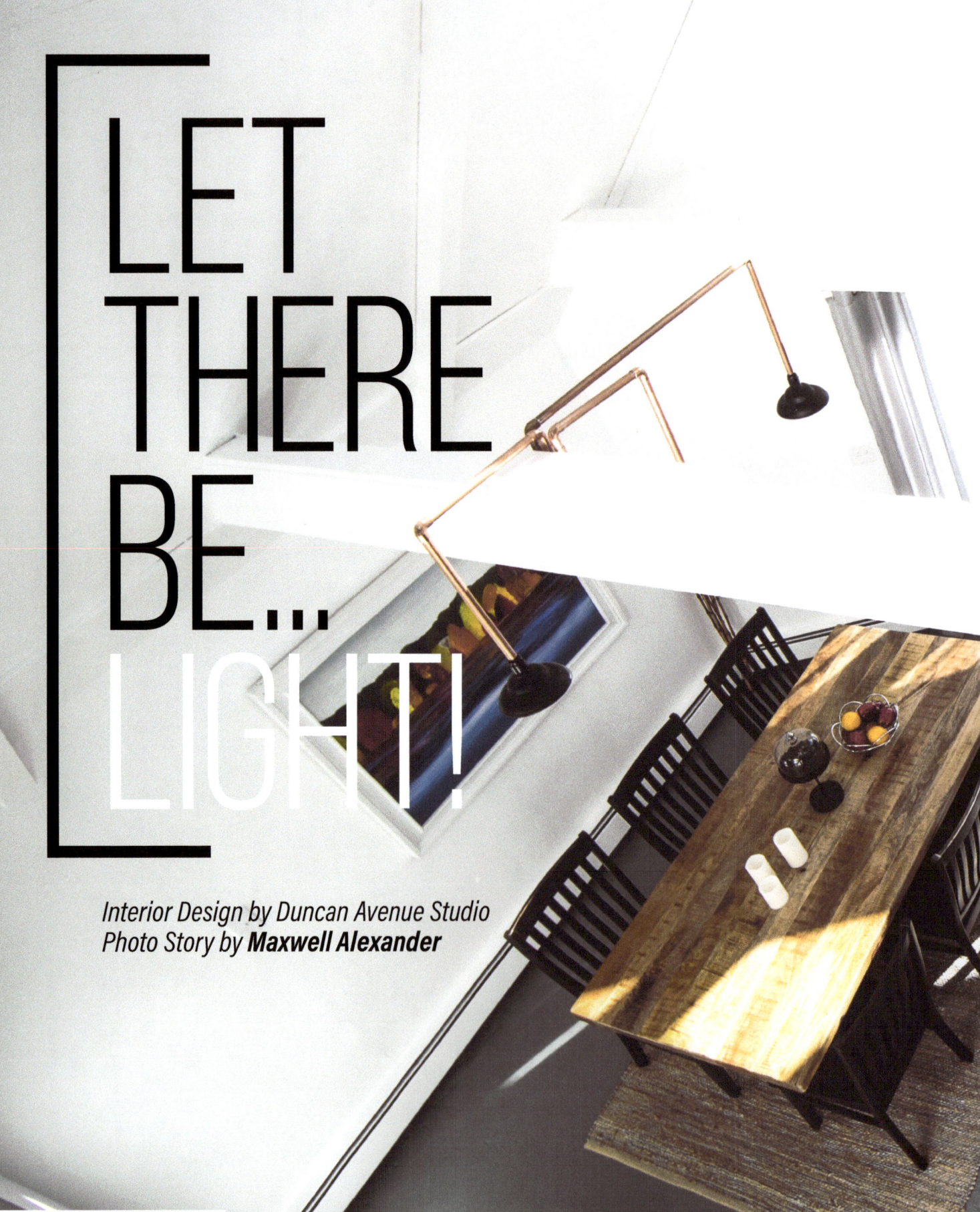

[HUDSON VALLEY STYLE LIVING]

[LET THERE BE... LIGHT!

Interior Design by Duncan Avenue Studio
Photo Story by **Maxwell Alexander**

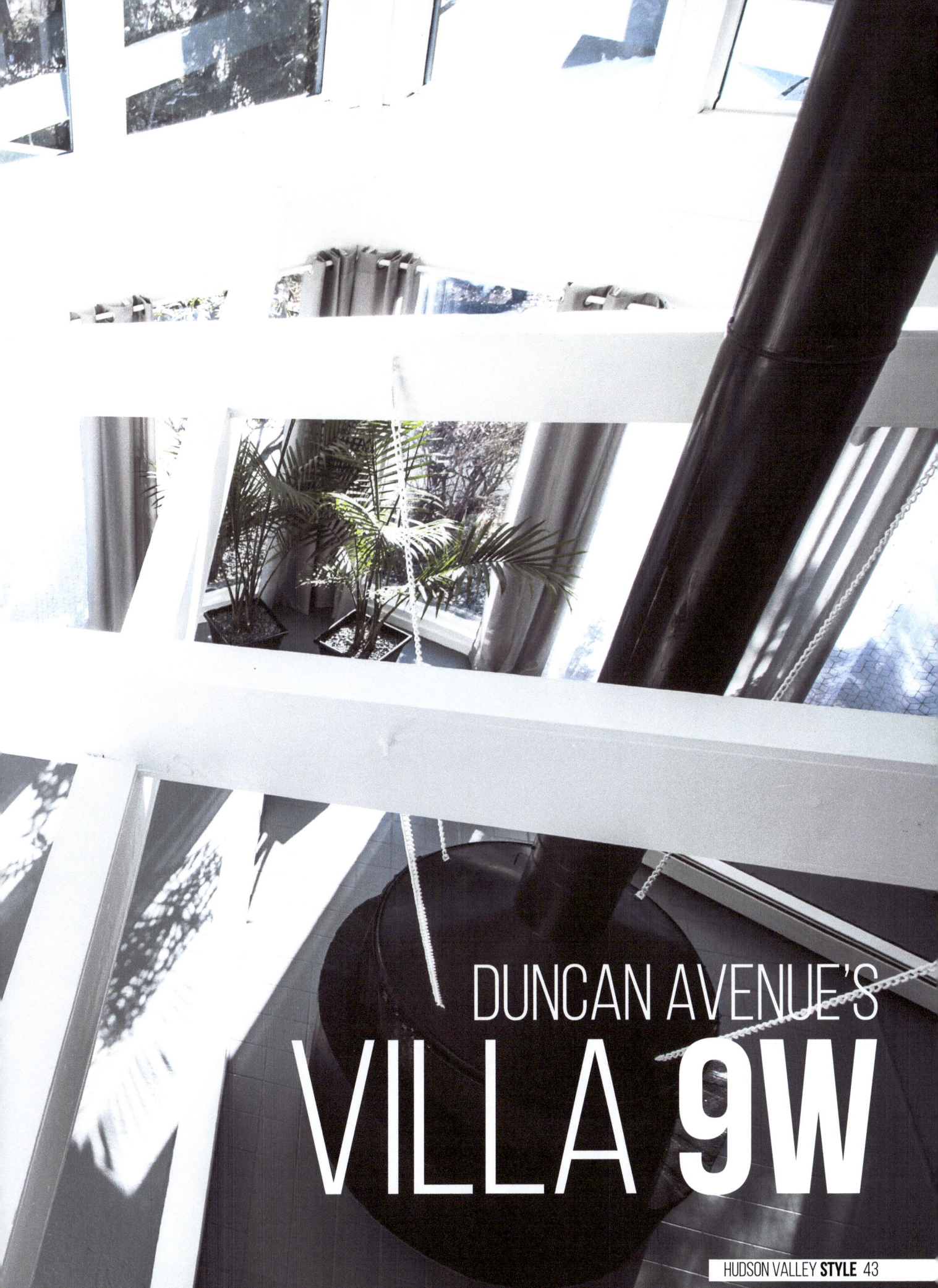

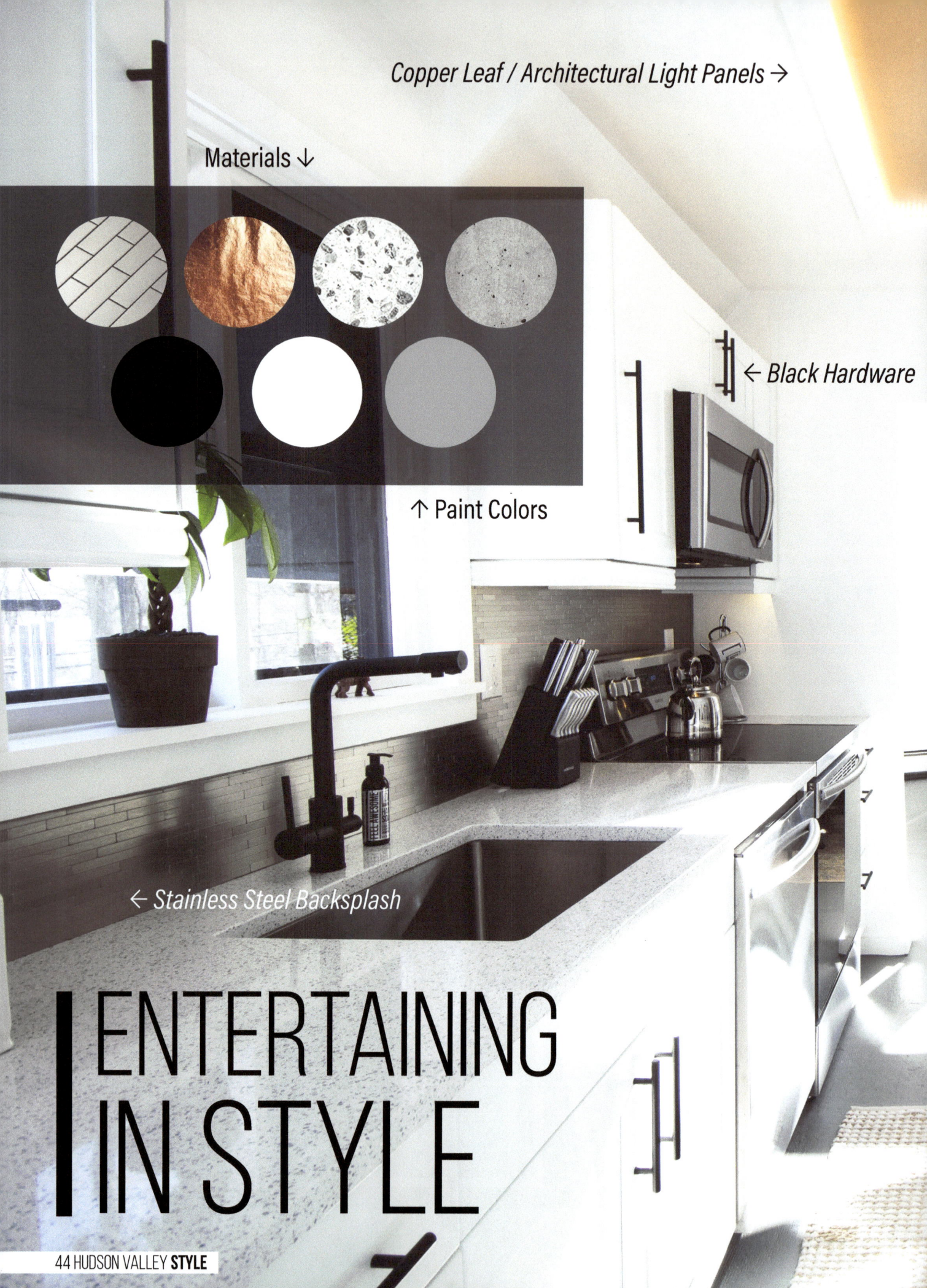

Copper Leaf / Architectural Light Panels →

Materials ↓

← Black Hardware

↑ Paint Colors

← Stainless Steel Backsplash

ENTERTAINING IN STYLE

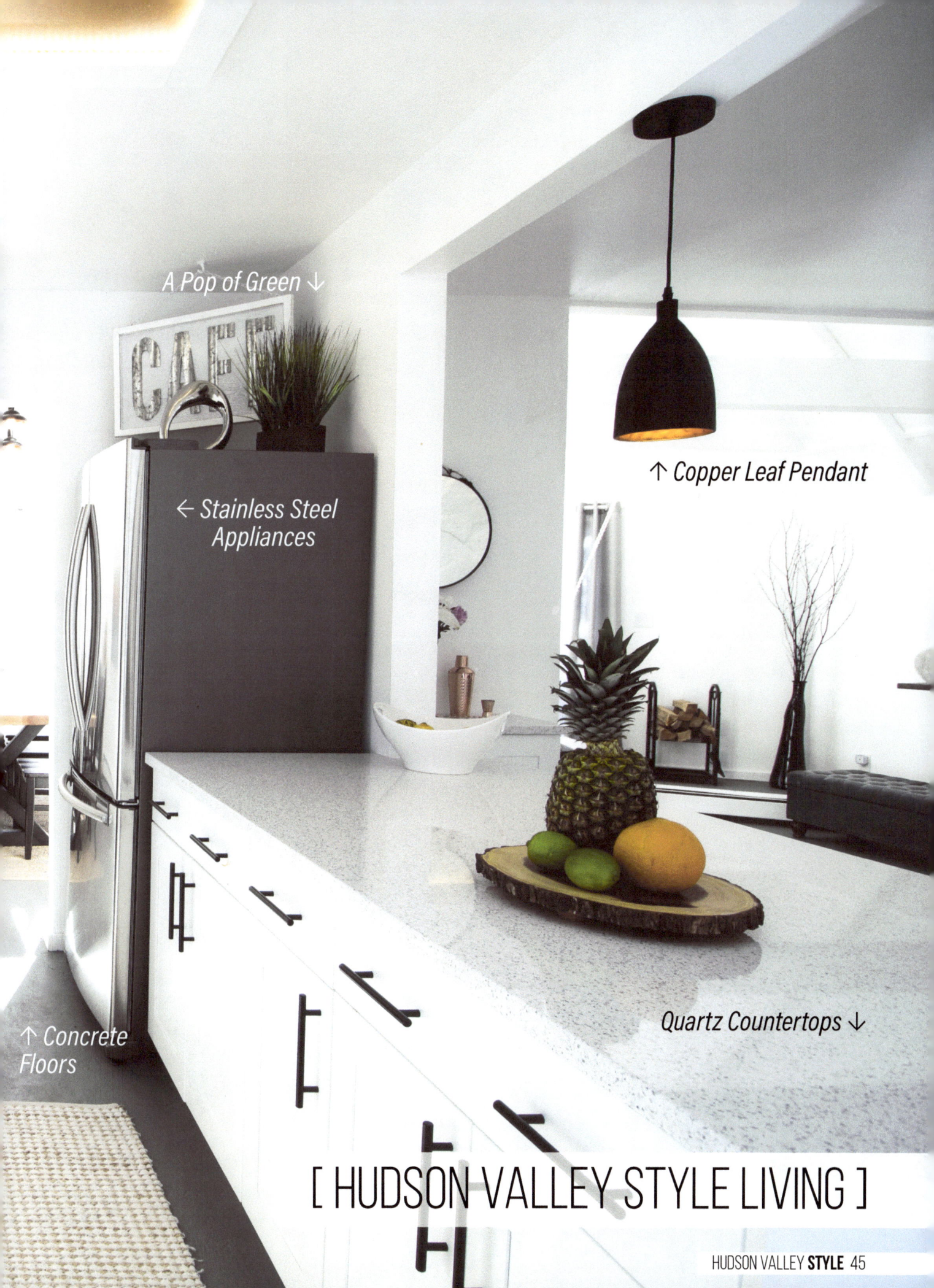

[HUDSON VALLEY STYLE LIVING]

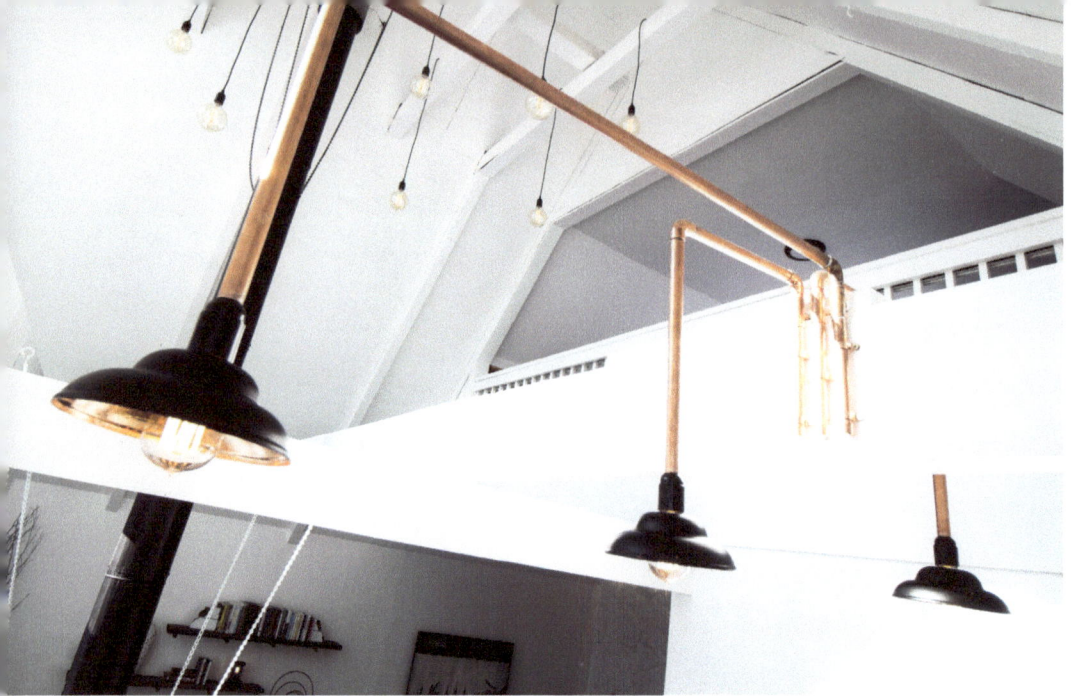

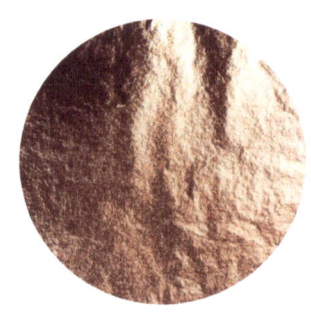

← *Custom Copper Lights*
© *Duncan Avenue Design*

White Granite Wall →

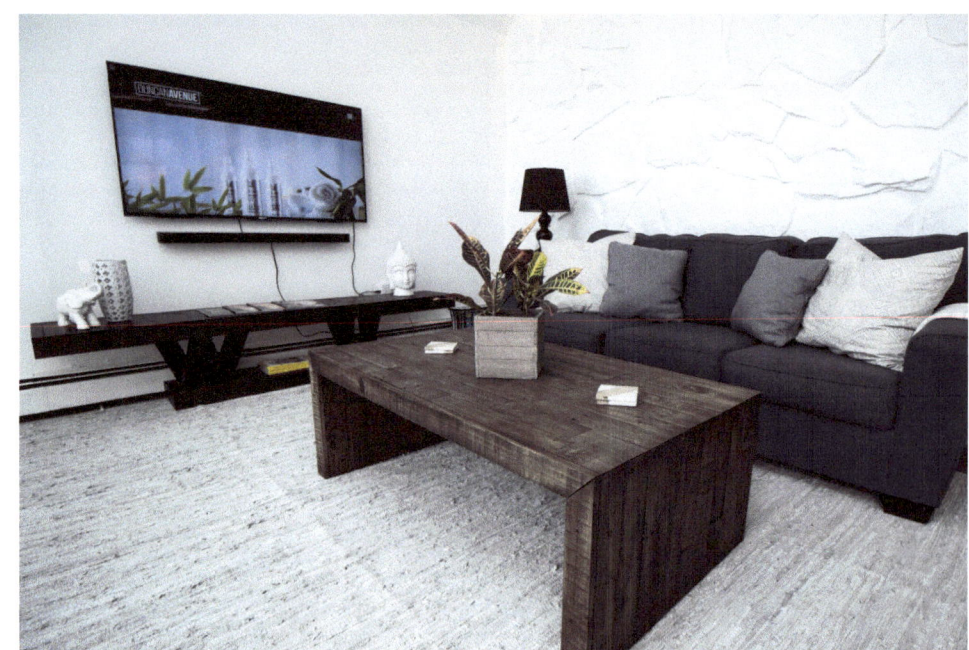

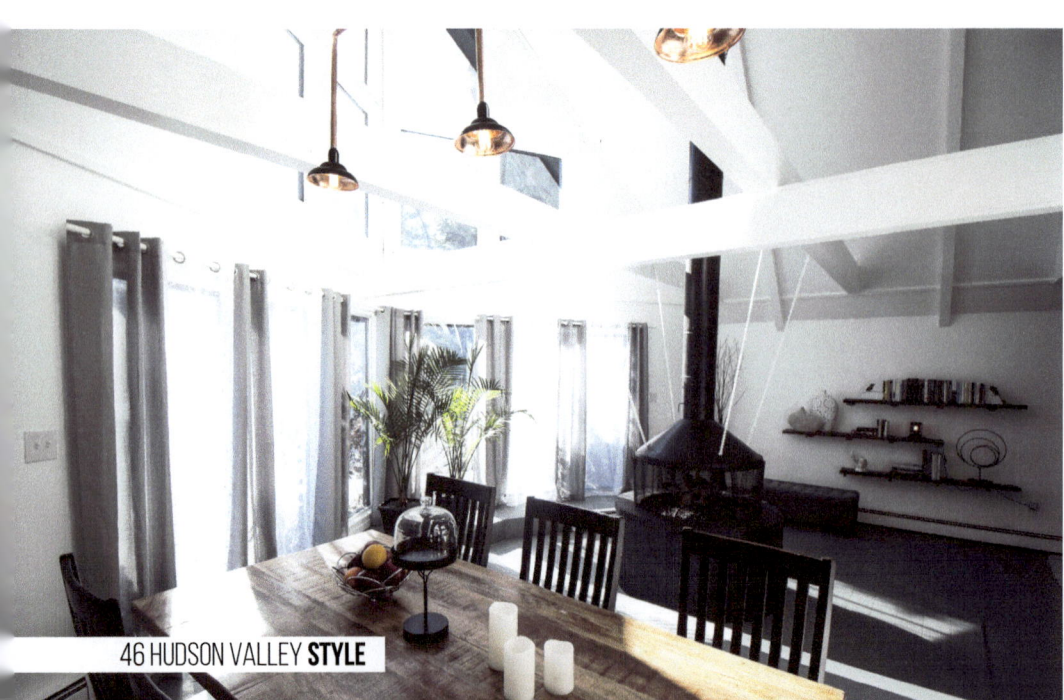

Wood Accents →

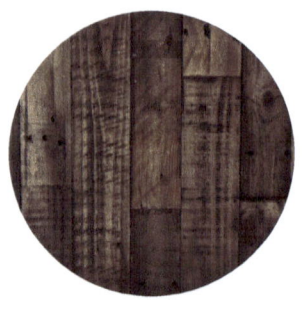

← *Formal Dining Area*

LIVING SPACE | WHITE BALANCE

Custom Entertainment
↓ *Console*

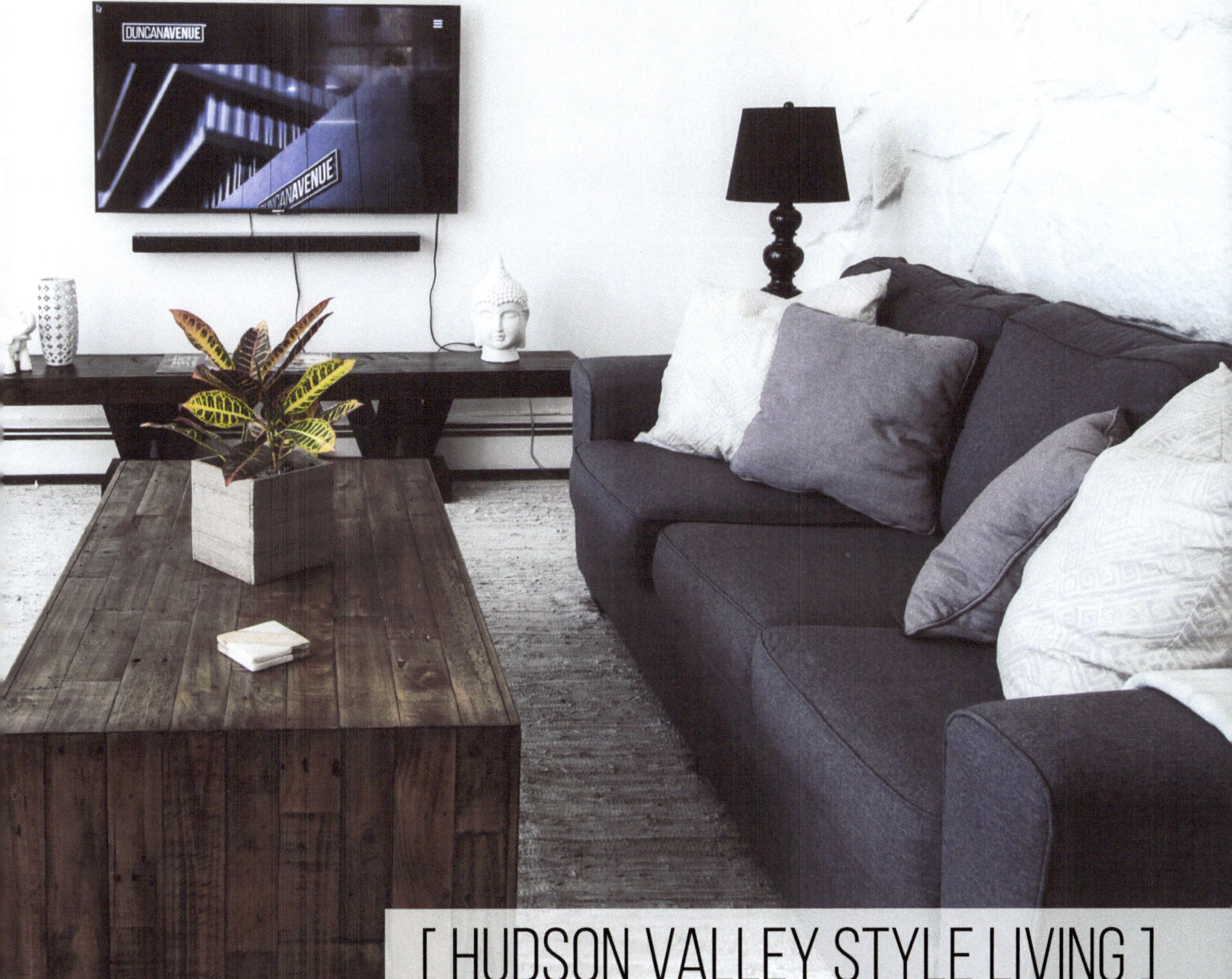

[HUDSON VALLEY STYLE LIVING]

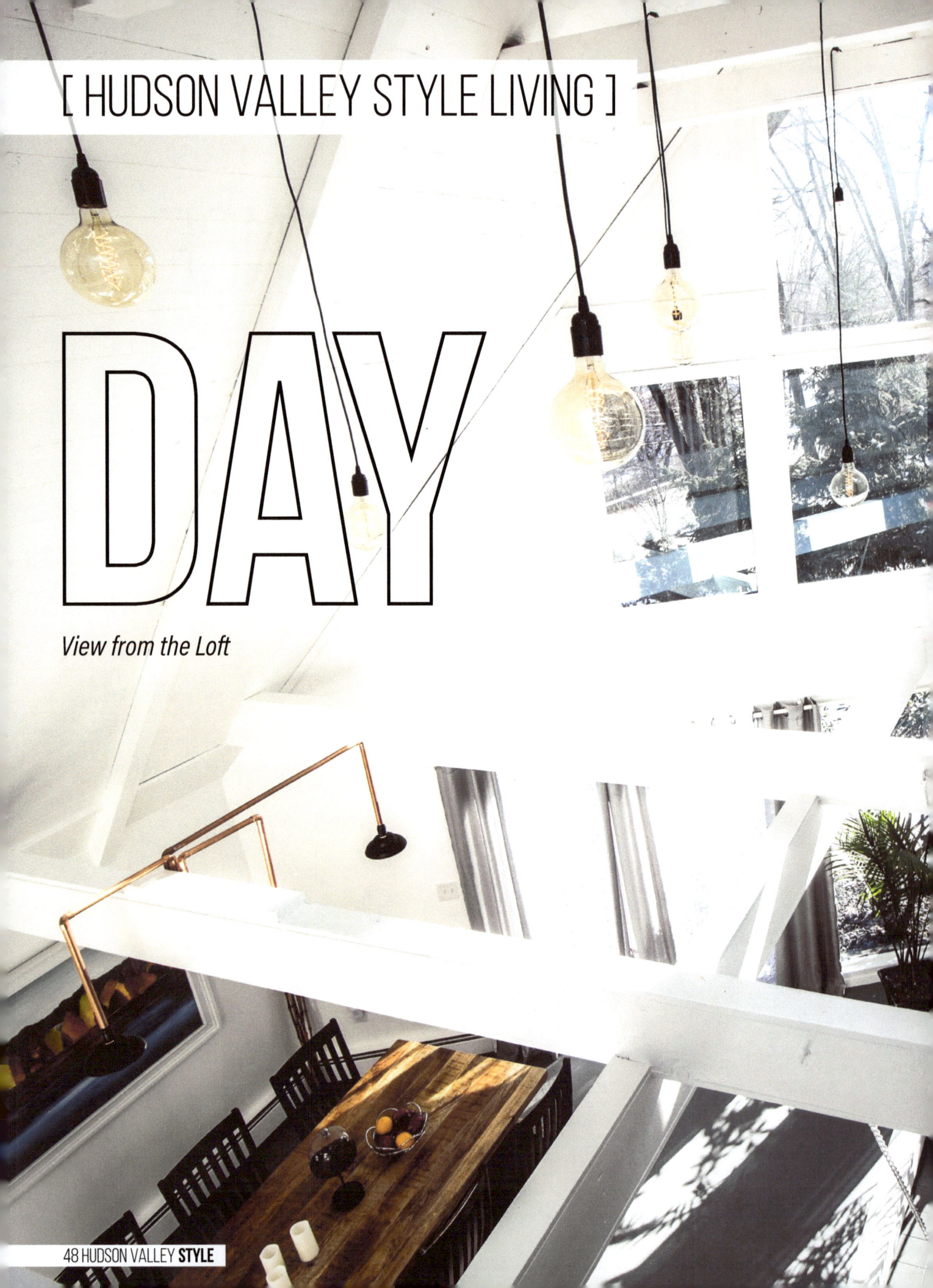

[HUDSON VALLEY STYLE LIVING]

DAY

View from the Loft

← 10 x 5" Edison Bulbs

VS
WARM

*Custom Light Fixture
by Duncan Avenue LightingDesign*

HUDSON VALLEY **STYLE** 49

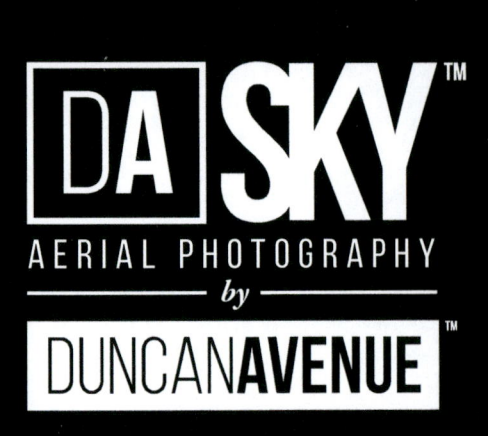

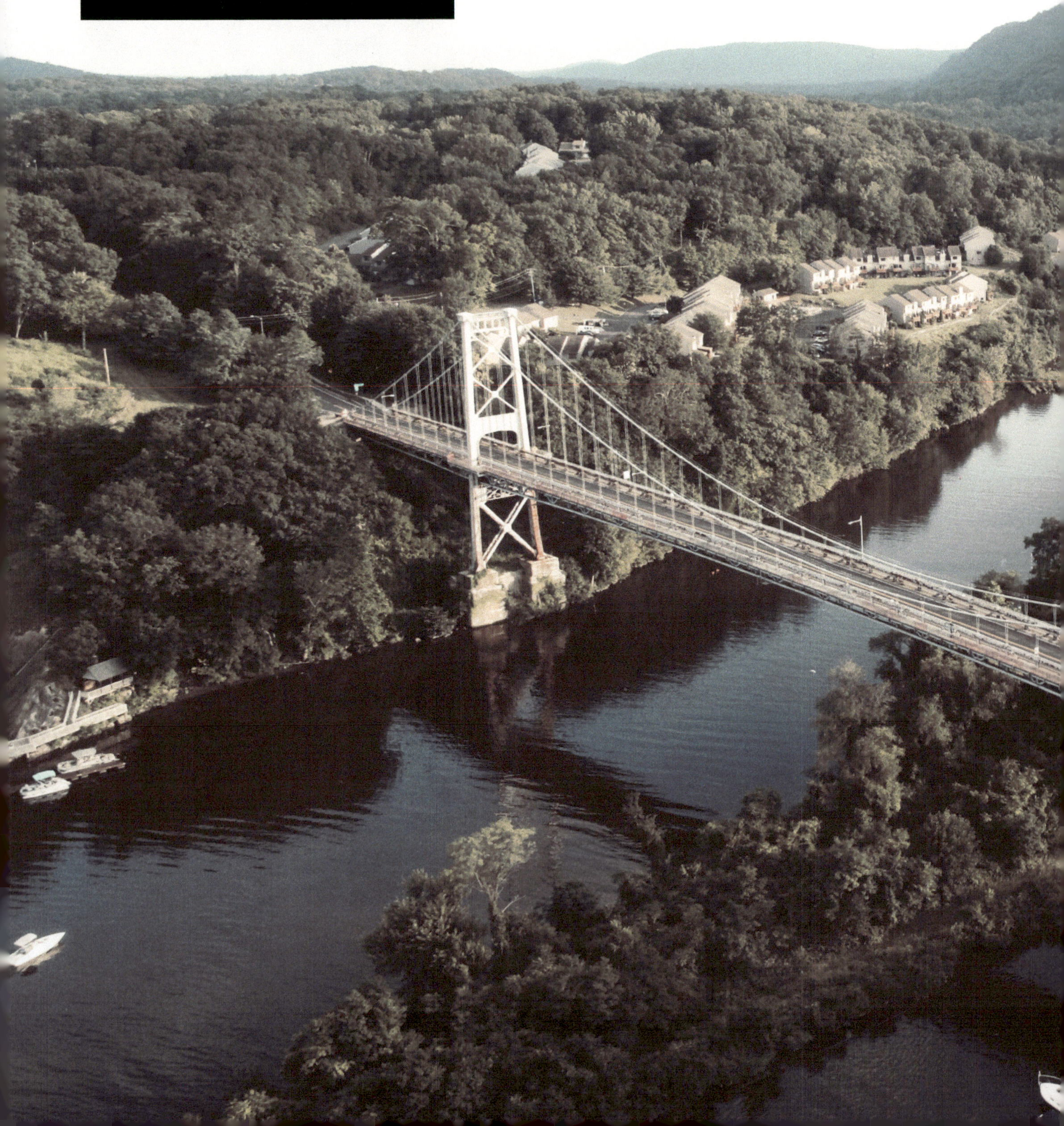

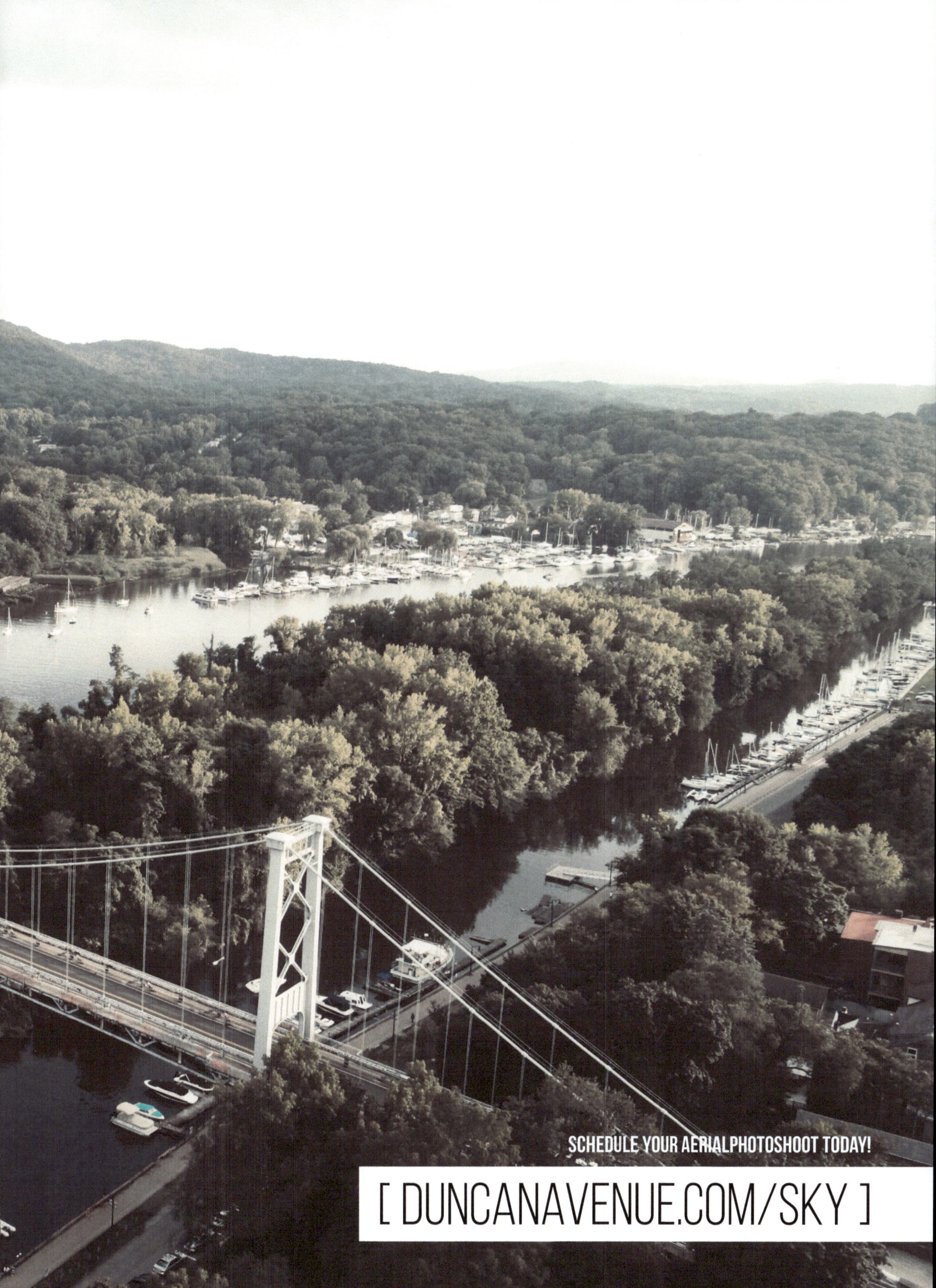

1-YEAR ONLINE BODYBUILDING PROGRAM
DESIGNER ★ ★BODY™
MAXWELL ALEXANDER .FITNESS

TECHNOLOGY-POWERED 24/7 TRAINING
1-Year Online or In-Person Bodybuilding Program

START YOUR JOURNEY TODAY!
Sign up at **MaxwellAlexander.Fitness**

WINTER ESSENTIALS

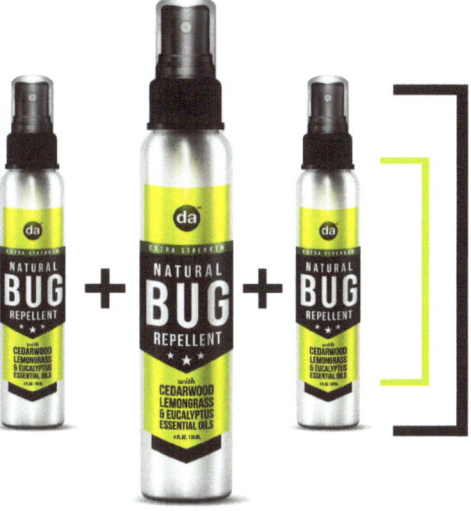

WOODLAND TRAILS BLEND
by DA Aromatherapy Collection

This natural insect repellent is made with 7 organic essential oils, it provides broad-spectrum protection and repels mosquitoes and ticks, fleas and many other pesky insects. The Best Natural Tick and Mosquito Repellent Spray is created for direct skin contact, safe for Humans and Pets and featuring exclusive Woodland Trails™ blend of Organic Lemongrass, Eucalyptus Lemon, and Eucalyptus Globulus, Cedarwood (Cedar Oil), Rosemary, Clove, and Lavender Essential Oils.

Our signature Tick and Mosquito Natural Spray will keep you sting and bite-free without the use of pesticides that are harmful to humans, the environment at large and especially good insects like honeybees. Our natural tick and mosquito repellent can help to protect you when sprayed in a room, on the balcony, in a car, on the body, and even on your clothes without staining.

DA-AROMATHERAPY.COM

$17.00

INSPIRING AROMATHERAPY MIST WITH ORGANIC LAVENDER AND SANDALWOOD ESSENTIAL OILS - WINDS OF STORMKING™
by DA Aromatherapy Collection

A luxurious and sensual fragrance of rich, woodsy sandalwood accord and beautiful flowery notes of lavender and spice. Winds of Stormking™ Essential Oil Blend perfectly captures the cool mountain breezes, sun sparkles in the Hudson River waters and lush foliage of the Hudson Valley.

DA-AROMATHERAPY.COM

$9.00

NATURAL HAND SANITIZERS WITH ORGANIC ESSENTIAL OILS
by DA Aromatherapy Collection

Working out at the gym or taking a Savasana on your yoga mat? Protect yourself and loved ones plus get an aromatherapy boost on the go with these natural hand sanitizers. DA Aromatherapy Hand Sanitizing Mists with Organic Essential Oils are effective against 99.9% of common germs and bacteria.

DA-AROMATHERAPY.COM

$9.00

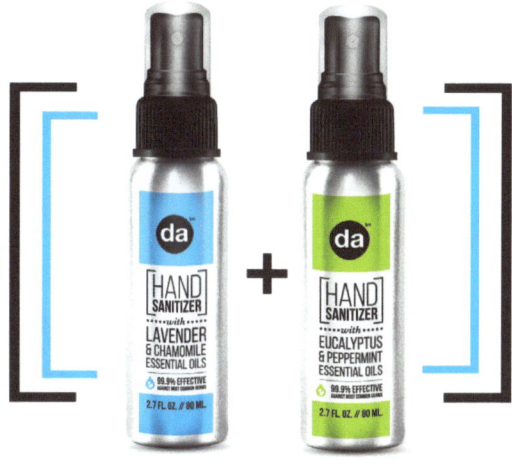

[da-aromatherapy.com]

KEEP NATURE NATURAL.

Our Natural Insect Repellents are made with Organic Essential Oils and are free of chemical pesticides that are harmful to your health and the environment.

da™ aromatherapy

FIVE MISTAKES THAT CAN RUIN YOUR FAT LOSS PLAN

by Certified Bodybuilding Trainer Maxwell Alexander

Every year, millions of people across the world attempt to lose weight. Many of them fail. If you would like to give your weight loss plan the best possible chance of success, you should try to avoid making any of the common mistakes that cause others to fail, such as:

NOT EATING ENOUGH

When attempting to shed those extra pounds, you may be tempted to skip meals or avoid eating for extended periods of time. Unfortunately, this approach is only likely to result in you feeling grumpy, lethargic, and desperate for a snack later in the day. To improve your odds of weight loss success, try to eat a healthy meal three times a day.

SETTING UNREALISTIC GOALS

As you begin your weight loss journey, you should set some goals for yourself. In doing so, however, you should ensure that your targets are attainable. If you set goals that are impossible to achieve, you are likely to feel down and unmotivated when you inevitably fail to meet them. As a result, you may decide to give up on your weight loss plan entirely.

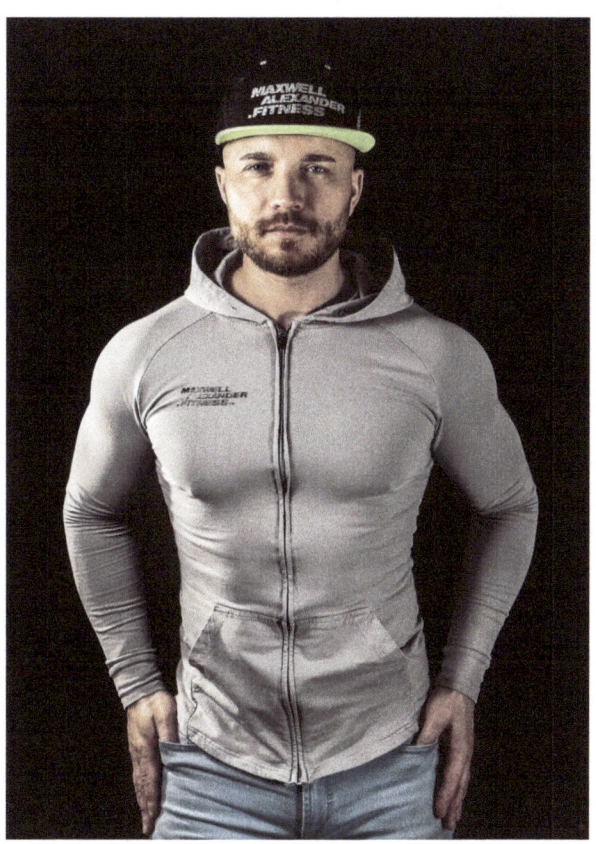

FAILING TO REWARD YOURSELF

As you accomplish your weight loss goals, you should take a moment to reward yourself for all your hard work. Of course, you should try to avoid using food as a reward. Instead, consider opting for new clothes or even a short vacation.

DOING THE SAME EXERCISES EVERY DAY

Exercising regularly can be a great way to lose some weight and improve your fitness. However, you should avoid becoming overly reliant on any one particular form of exercise. If your workouts are the same every day, you are likely to get bored of them very quickly. To keep yourself interested and engaged, mix up your exercise plan as much as possible.

NOT GETTING ENOUGH SLEEP

When it comes to weight loss, sleep has many benefits. First and foremost, it provides your body with a chance to recover from the rigors of the day, something which is particularly useful if you have an intense workout schedule. It also re-energizes you for the following day and can speed up your metabolism. In short, if you are not getting enough shuteye, you are likely to find it difficult to lose weight.

IN CLOSING

Losing weight can be challenging. However, it does not have to be impossible. As long as you keep working hard and avoid making the mistakes outlined above, you should notice those extra pounds begin to drop off before too long. If you still need help, I have an awesome Weight Loss Program just for you! Working with one of the Best Online Fitness Coaches like myself, you can get better results in a shorter period of time, so why not give it a try? Log on to MaxwellAlexander.Fitness to learn more about my Online Weight Loss Coaching Program.

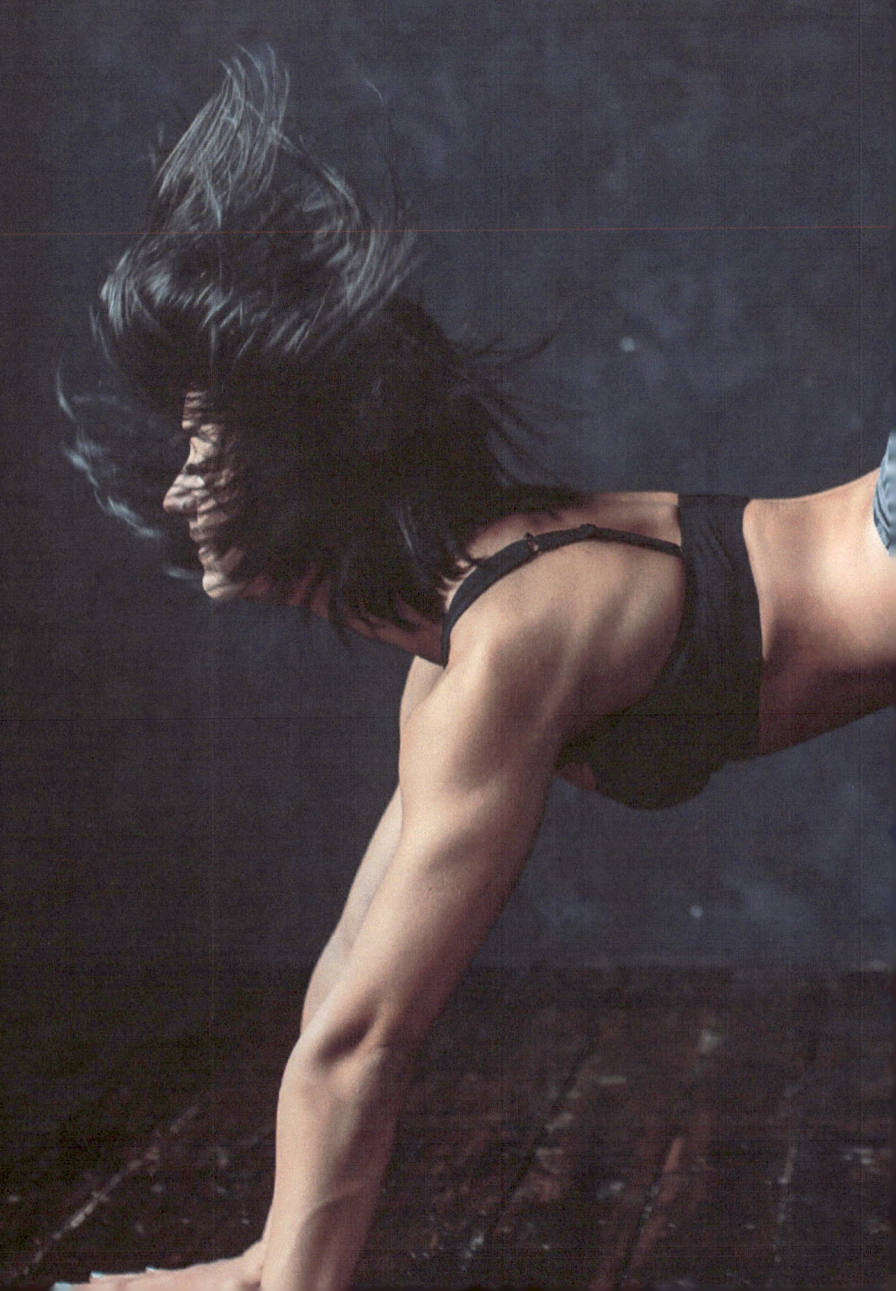

The way people buy and sell things has inherently changed in the last decade. Why should real estate be any different? The industry as you know it is lagging dreadfully behind, but Almax Realty is disrupting the system with a bold, new outlook on what is necessary to become a successful real estate agent.

CUTTING-EDGE ENVIRONMENT

Contrary to the notion that we're all lazy and entitled, Millennials are overtaking the workforce and the real estate market. Alexander Maxwell Realty understands your need for a cutting-edge environment to thrive in. We're not talking about gimmicks like bean bags and espresso bars; we are talking about a technology-powered system designed for agents that operate differently—a system that enables you to succeed.

THE OPPORTUNITY IS IN THE FIELD

As a matter of fact, the less you see our office, the better, even though it's a beautiful office. We do not require you to waste time on senseless, hierarchical office duties because the opportunity is in the field. You get what you put in, and with a flexible schedule that allows you to work as much or as little as you'd like, not a minute is wasted. Our agency is not the old boy's club that you know so well. We think of ourselves as business partners, providing you with all the tools it takes to go from showing to closing, to an unrivaled commission check in your bank account.

WORLD-CLASS MARKETING

At Almax Realty, our agents are always moving forward. Our commission structure is based on a true buyer's agent 90-10 split, with no extra charges or fees. We are not in the business of thievery. We strive to invest in our agents from day one by providing honest commission for honest work, and an arsenal of world-class marketing materials to help you build strong client relationships. From complimentary, strategic marketing packages to award-winning photography, we have your back.

CONTROL YOUR DESTINY

Alexander Maxwell Realty is a platform where you control your destiny and your career, and we want to do everything we can to help you reach your goals. Support and innovation are the pillars on which that platform lies, and our core values transcend the hollow text on a mission statement. We have a growing team of highly motivated, like-minded agents and we are always looking for more, so just drop us a line to get started!

LEARN MORE & APPLY TO JOIN AT ALMAXREALTY.COM

#FRESH
#AMBITIOUS
#VICTORIOUS
#JOINUS

[REAL ESTATE STYLE]

JOIN HUDSON VALLEY'S BEST REAL ESTATE AGENCY

BY DINO ALEXANDER
CEO, ALEXANDER MAXWELL REALTY

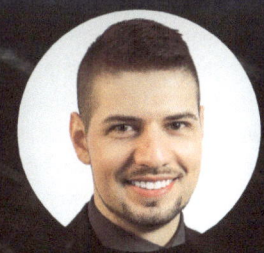

AERIAL PHOTOGRAPHY IN THE HUDSON VALLEY

by Maxwell Alexander

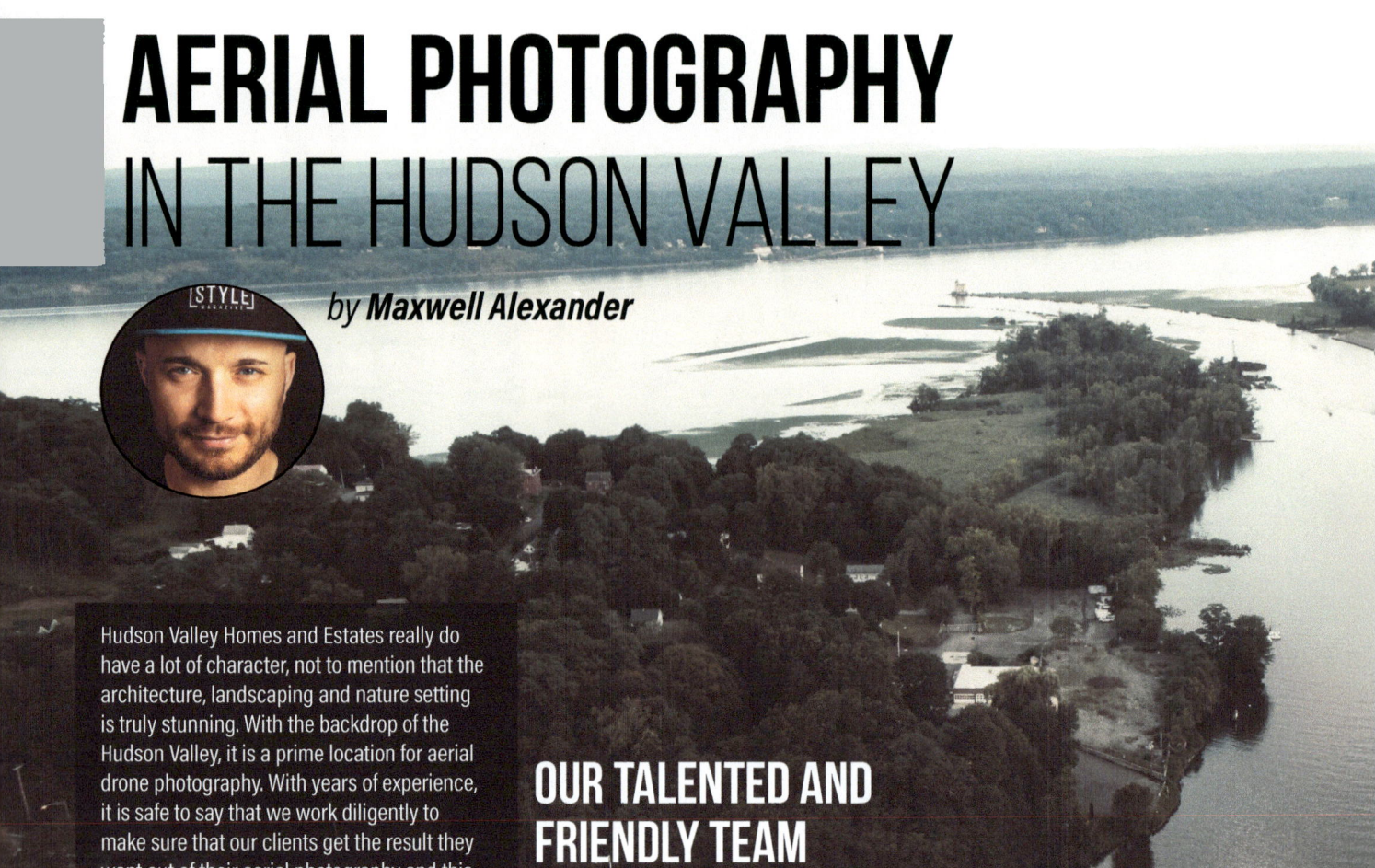

Hudson Valley Homes and Estates really do have a lot of character, not to mention that the architecture, landscaping and nature setting is truly stunning. With the backdrop of the Hudson Valley, it is a prime location for aerial drone photography. With years of experience, it is safe to say that we work diligently to make sure that our clients get the result they want out of their aerial photography and this is especially the case if they are trying to sell or market their property. With breath-taking photographs and a friendly team who will work closely with you every single step of the way, you know that you can count on us to go that extra mile while also delivering remarkable and stylish photos that you never thought possible.

HARNESSING THE POWER & BEAUTY OF NATURE

We know that nature is truly a force to be reckoned with, but in the right situation, it can also provide you with the perfect setting for an inspiring photo shoot. It doesn't matter whether it is sunset, sunrise, in the middle of a heatwave or snowing like it's Christmas Day because we have the ability to use every situation to your advantage. This means that we capture photographs like you have never seen before and it also means that the end result won't be like every other real estate photography out there.

OUR TALENTED AND FRIENDLY TEAM

Led by Maxwell Alexander, World-Class Art Director and Photographer, our team knows exactly how to approach a luxury property with flawless execution. We take into account the style of the home, the surrounding greenery and more, before planning our angle of approach and camera view. This gives us the chance to capture your home in the best possible way while also giving us the chance to provide every single viewer (your potential buyer) with a unique and magical experience.

OUR DRONES AND PILOTS

When you come to us for all of your drone photography needs and requirements, you'll find that we have the latest professional equipment and only FAA-licensed drone pilots. Not only does this mean that we are able to deliver a better result than our competitors, but it also means that we have the experience you need to really stand out from the crowd.

OUR SPECTACULAR AERIAL REAL ESTATE PHOTOGRAPHY

Aerial Photography is one of the best ways to highlight your Real Estate Property including indoor and outdoor photo and video shots. We can cover landscape features and look and feel of the neighborhood, all of it is important to your potential buyers.

If you are interested in our team, how we can help you or even to see if there is anything that we can do for you then please do get in touch with us today. We would love to hear from you and we are very excited to work with you to get you the best result out of your aerial photography.

Review Our Aerial Photography Portfolio and Schedule Your Aerial Photo Shoot at DuncanAvenue.com

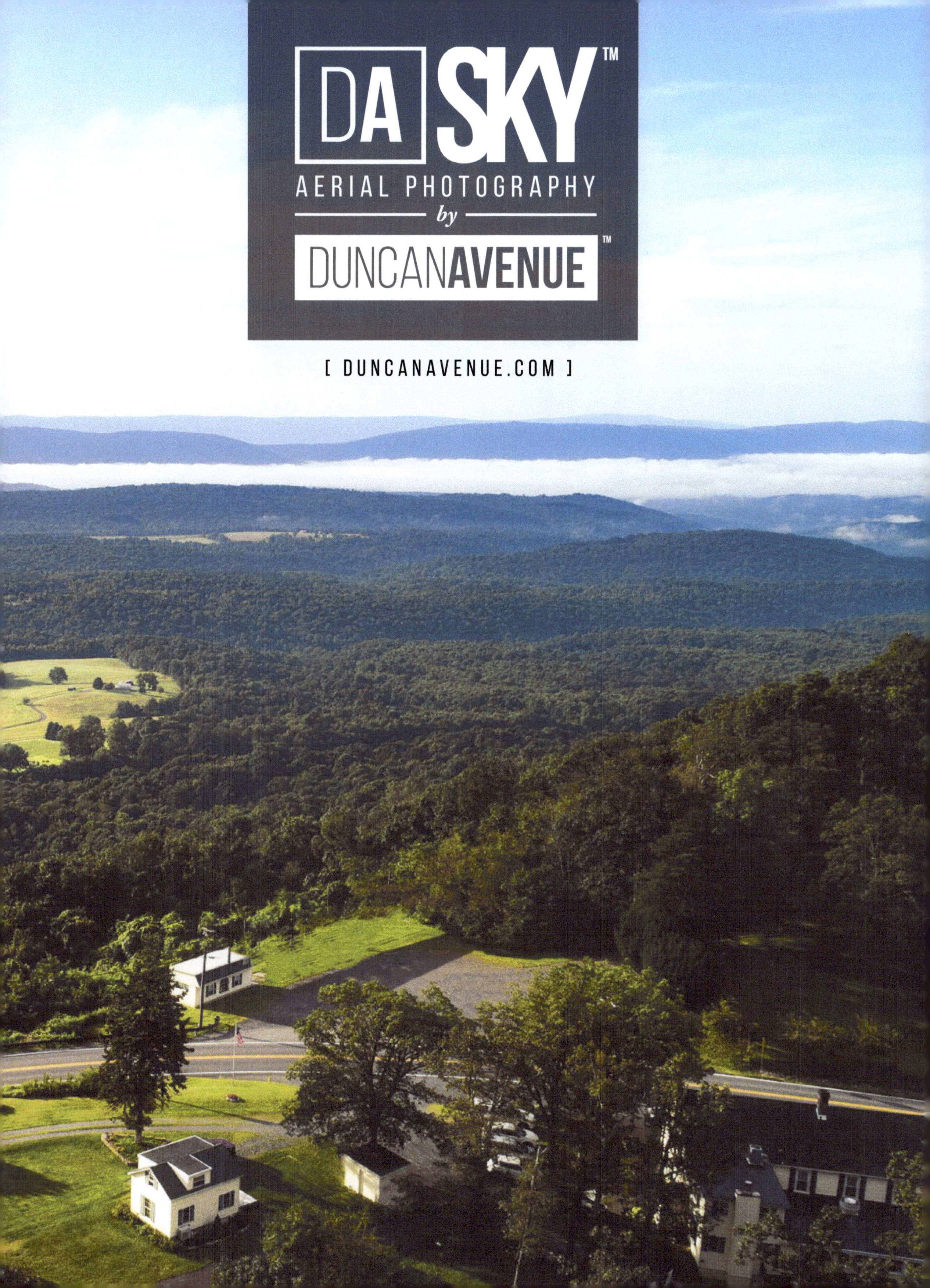

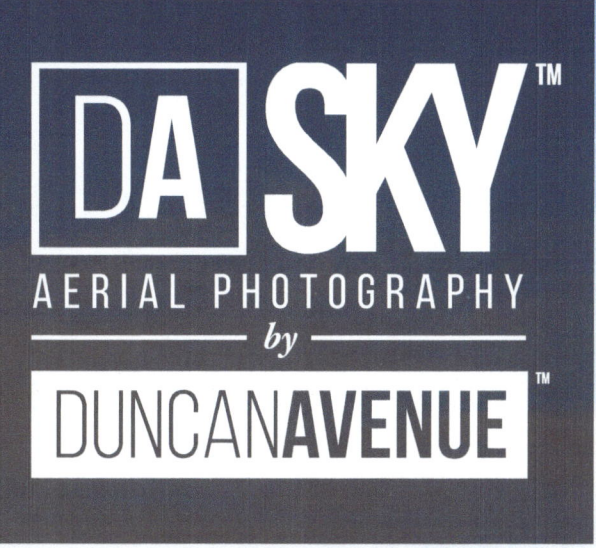

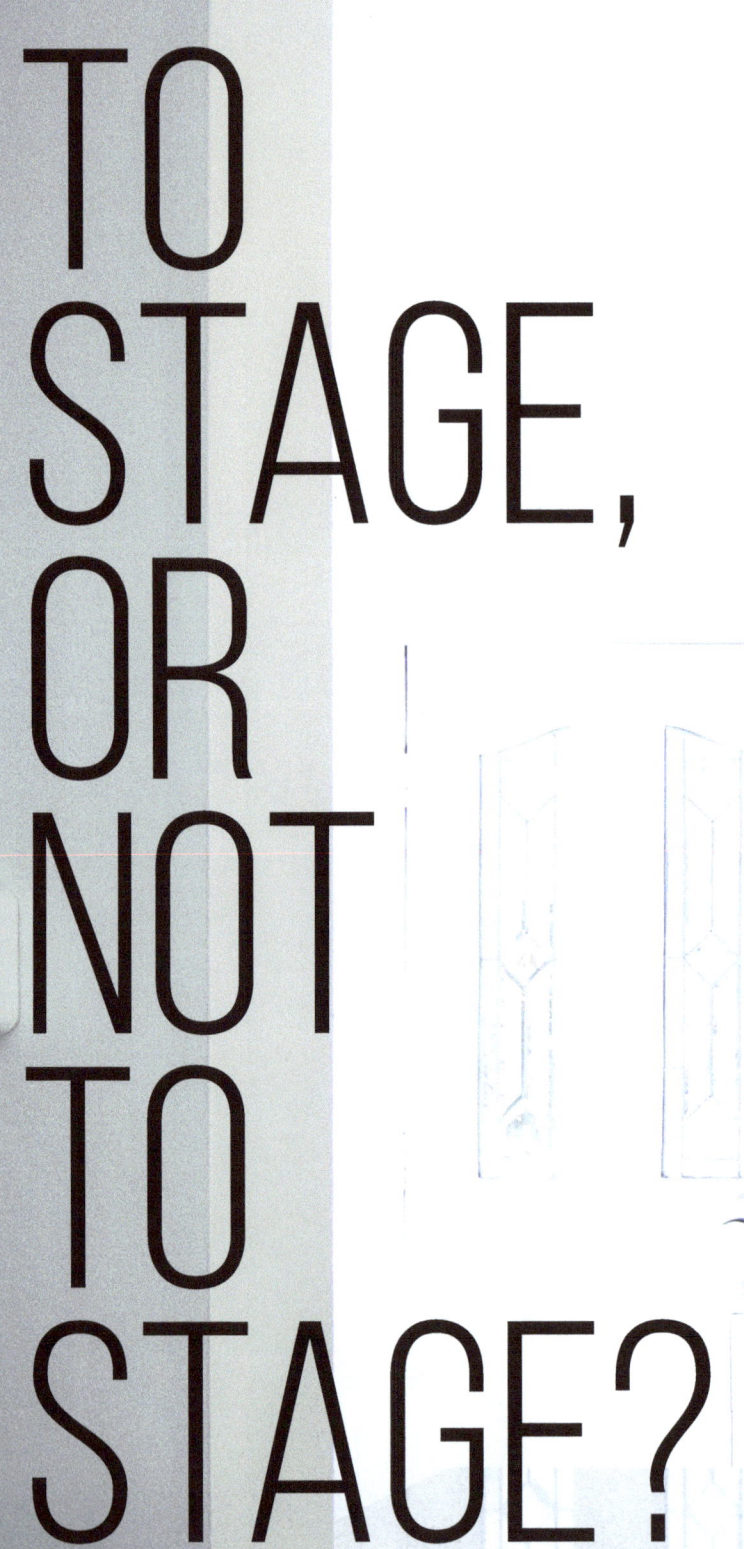

TO STAGE, OR NOT TO STAGE?

Learn More about this design project →
at duncanavenue.com/design

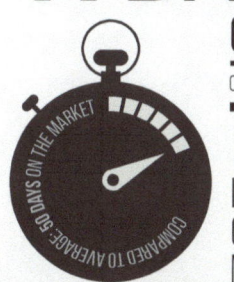

PORTRAIT OF A PERFUMER
BY HELENA PALAZZI

[PHOTOGRAPHY & FASHION EDITOR]
HELENAPALAZZI.COM

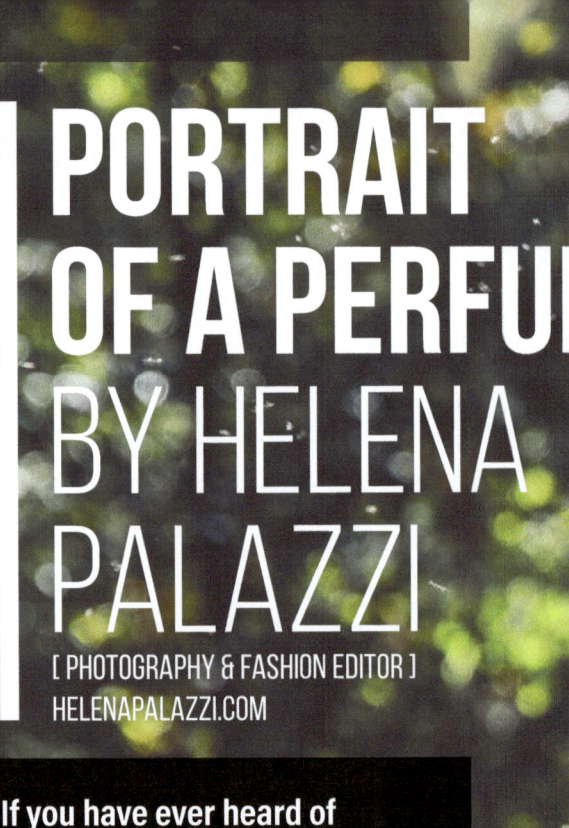

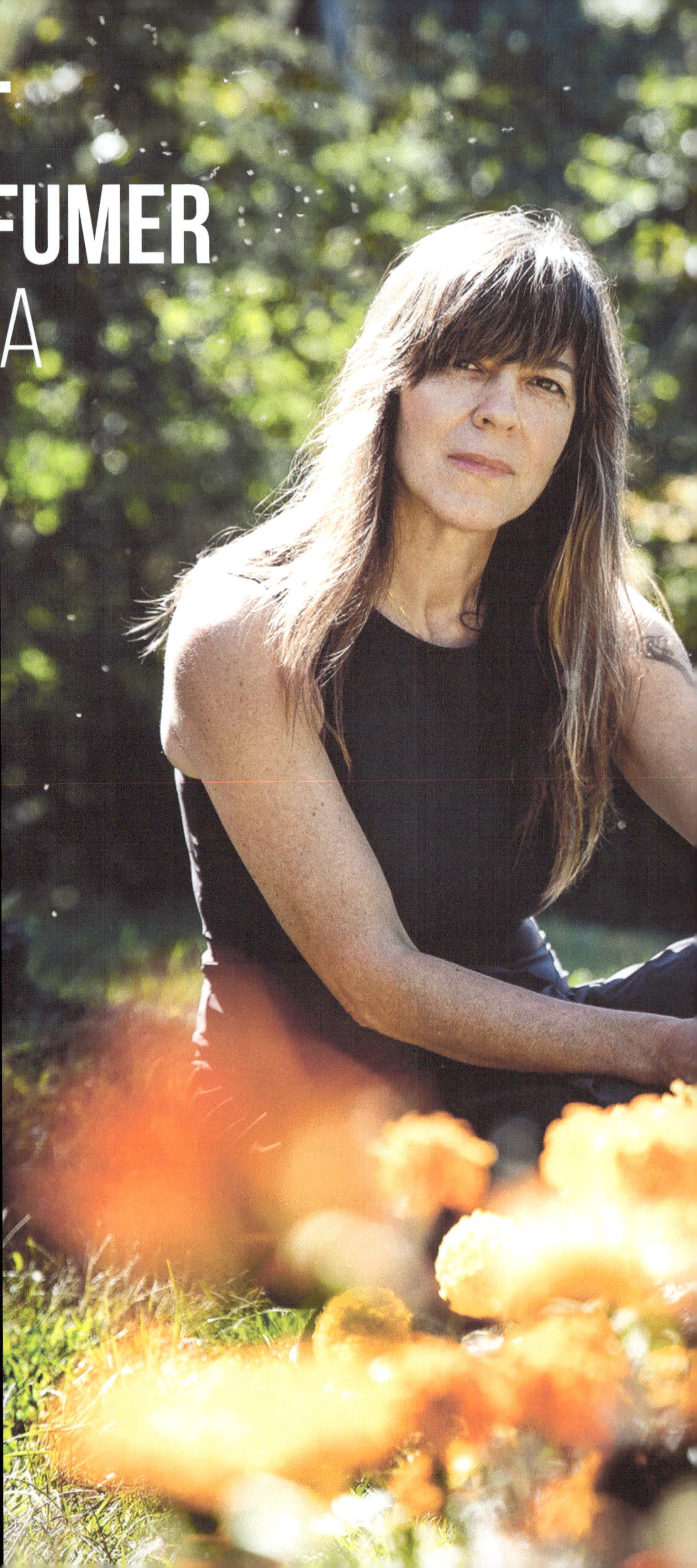

If you have ever heard of or read Marcel Proust "Remembrance of all Things Past" you are most likely also familiar with the famous passage where he recalls long-forgotten childhood memories from one tiny bite and smell of a madeleine cookie.

The first time I was invited into Janette Bower's study, where her compositions come together, I was allowed to sample one of her perfumes in the making. Upon my first scent, I was immediately brought back to my own childhood; remembering my mother and her ever-present large purse where she kept various mysterious items such as a small flowery bottle of perfume, a tube of lotion and peppermint candy.

This is the power of the olfactory and in addition to being the sense most closely linked to memory, the smell is also highly emotive. The smell is extremely important when it comes to attraction between people. Kissing is in fact thought by some scientists to have developed from sniffing; that first kiss being essentially a primal behavior during which we smell and taste our partner to decide if they are a match.

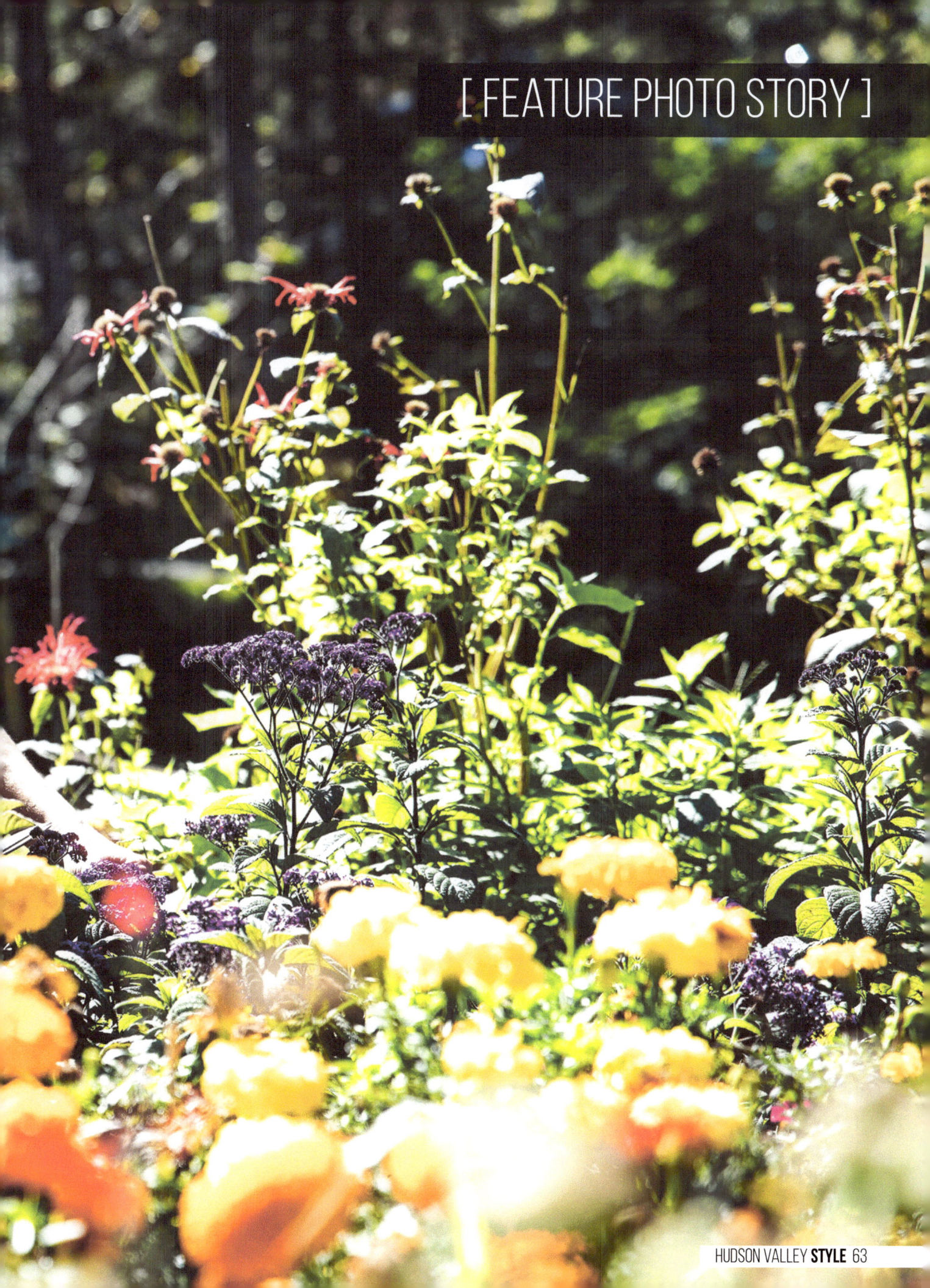

[PORTRAIT OF A PERFUMER]
BY HELENA PALAZZI

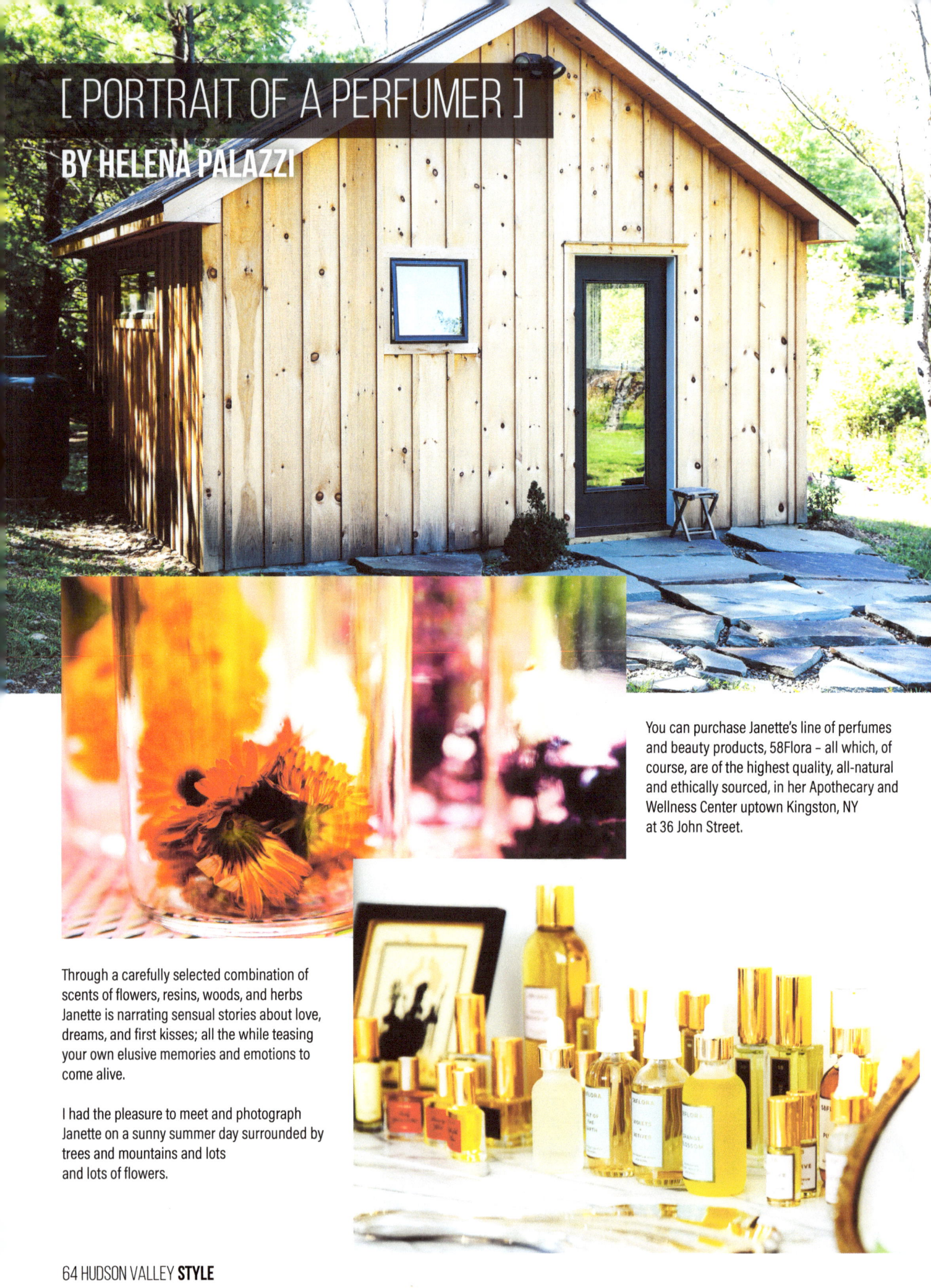

You can purchase Janette's line of perfumes and beauty products, 58Flora – all which, of course, are of the highest quality, all-natural and ethically sourced, in her Apothecary and Wellness Center uptown Kingston, NY at 36 John Street.

Through a carefully selected combination of scents of flowers, resins, woods, and herbs Janette is narrating sensual stories about love, dreams, and first kisses; all the while teasing your own elusive memories and emotions to come alive.

I had the pleasure to meet and photograph Janette on a sunny summer day surrounded by trees and mountains and lots and lots of flowers.

www.ingramcontent.com/pod-product-compliance
Lightning Source LLC
Chambersburg PA
CBHW051207220526
45473CB00003B/935